101

Grade A

Résumés

for Teachers

by Rebecca Anthony and Gerald Roe

BARRON'S

ABOUT THE AUTHORS

Rebecca Jespersen Anthony and Gerald Roe are career specialists in placement at The University of Iowa. In addition to numerous articles, they have published six books.

Rebecca Anthony is a recent president of the Association for School, College and University Staffing, a national organization for placement professionals and school administrators, and a past president of Great Lakes Association for School, College and University Staffing.

Information for the section on teachers in Canada was contributed by AlanTravers (B.A., M.Ed.), Placement Director at the Faculty of Education, Queen's University, Kingston, Ontario, Canada.

FOR

Natalya, Tassie, Veronica

Steve, April, Dave

Anthony, Allison

All inquiries should be addressed to:
Barron's Educational Series, Inc.
250 Wireless Boulevard
Hauppauge, New York 11788

Library of Congress Catalog Card No.: 93-34894

International Standard Book No. 0-8120-1810-9

Library of Congress Cataloging-in-Publication Data
Anthony, Rebecca, 1950–
    101 Grade A résumés for teachers / by Rebecca Anthony & Gerald Roe.
     p. cm.
    ISBN 0-8120-1810-9
    1. Teachers—Employment. 2. Résumés (Employment) 3. Cover letters. I. Roe, Gerald.
    II. Title. III. Title: One hundred one grade A résumés for teachers.
LB 1780.A68 1994
808'.06665—dc20   93-34894
                             CIP

PRINTED IN THE UNITED STATES OF AMERICA
  56 100 987654

CONTENTS

PREFACE

Books about résumés are numerous and readily available.

Why yet another résumé book?

Why, above all, a book of résumés for teachers?

Existing résumé books are filled with advice and examples for job seekers in a wide variety of occupations. But educators who look into these books do not find themselves reflected there. Even though the teaching profession numbers more than 2.5 million people with more than a hundred thousand new graduates per year eligible to join the ranks, no résumé book has addressed their special interests or requirements. For educators, a résumé is not only a job search tool; it is an ongoing record of professional development submitted for merit or tenure reviews, grant applications, or to support candidacy for leadership positions in regional or national associations.

A teacher's résumé is only superficially like résumés in the business sector. Educators have different needs, even a different vocabulary. Teachers and school administrators cannot rely on numbers to document efficiency or percentage increases to prove productivity. Promotion is not an issue and profitability must never be the bottom line.

Our experience with thousands of teachers over the past twenty years has given us the opportunity to work with beginning and experienced teachers in almost every possible circumstance. Whether they are beginners displaying their shiny new qualifications or seasoned professionals attempting to distill a lifetime accumulation of experiences, helping them to promote themselves on paper has been for us both a challenge and a reward. We are confident that if you look into this book, you will see your career reflected.

PART ONE

YOUR
RESUME

1

WHAT IS A RESUME?

A résumé is a summary of experience. That's all it is, just a summary of experience. It is not a technical blueprint, an autobiography, a testament, or an essay. A résumé is not a legal document, nor is it a formal declaration prepared according to standard specifications. It is a summary of experience—period.

Yet most people think writing a résumé is going to be difficult. Consequently, they worry about it—

> they procrastinate—
> they seek advice from friends or family—
> they copy the first model they see, or—
> they get someone to do it for them.

Many people mistakenly think they need a professional résumé writer, someone who has acquired a superior knowledge of the elaborate science and intricate mechanics of résumé construction.

The truth is, *you* are the expert. You are the person best qualified to put yourself on paper. Considering the importance of a résumé in today's marketplace, you would be foolish to allow anyone else to do it for you. No one can do it better.

Even if you are just beginning your career in education, you have found many occasions to create a paper profile. You filled out applications to be admitted to college and more forms to enter a teacher preparation program. You know how to provide information to the Internal Revenue Service, a bank, a financial aid office, a credit card company. You could almost consider yourself an expert at filling out forms.

Unfortunately, you may never escape the struggle to fit the shape of your life into a form of someone else's devising. But preparing a résumé is less complicated and far more interesting than merely filling out forms. In the first place, *you* get to decide what's most important. You decide what you want to highlight; you even decide what you'd just as soon not call to anyone's attention. You control the presentation, you design the format, and you create your best professional image.

THE GREAT RESUME MYTH:
FITTING INTO PRESCRIPTIVE MODELS

Over the years, résumés have been forced to fit neatly or awkwardly into prescribed models. In any library, there are many, many books about writing résumés, but they do not meet the needs of educators. Many of the books describe two principal types of résumés: *chronological and functional.* Some writers include lengthy discussions of the differences between these two types of résumés, and the advantages and disadvantages inherent in each

Briefly, a chronological résumé takes a historical approach. The résumé focuses on dates and locations, listing educational background and work record, including job titles and names of employers. A functional résumé, on the other hand, emphasizes competencies, abilities, and achievements without necessarily relating them to a specific work experience or time frame.

Too often, strict adherence to either model will limit an educator's ability to make the most advantageous presentation. Each model has features that can capture the reader's attention and promote specific strengths. The most effective features of chronological and functional approaches can be combined in a résumé that emphasizes your unique personal and professional attributes.

No single prescribed model should dictate the format, arrangement, or organization of your résumé. Common sense, combined with your particular priorities, should be the hallmark of your presentation.

2
EDUCATORS NEED RESUMES

Only a generation or so ago, comparatively few people prepared or even knew about résumés. There was no need to bother about a résumé; it wasn't necessary, it wasn't expected, and it just wasn't a standard operating procedure. In academic circles, a college professor would routinely prepare a specialized résumé, called a *curriculum vitae*, as a record of academic and professional accomplishments. Most other people were unfamiliar with the practice or the concept.

A number of events and circumstances have precipitated change. Federal and state legislation supports the idea of equal employment opportunities for all people. Jobs are widely advertised and competition for available positions is often intense, with the number of qualified applicants far exceeding the number of vacancies. In today's climate, a résumé is an essential document for:

- student teachers
- first-year teachers
- experienced teachers

And for:

- substitute teachers
- paraprofessionals

And for:

- supervisors
- consultants
- principals
- superintendents.

Whether you are a novice or a veteran, if you are or if you want to become one of these educators, you need a résumé.

DIFFERENT STROKES...

Like professionals in many other fields—marketing, finance, engineering, medicine, science, government, and social service—educators need to know how to prepare and use a résumé. But different professions require different approaches, different treatments, different vocabularies. A résumé must be particularly suited to the profession as well as to the individual. A model résumé for a marketing director will be of no help to a third grade teacher.

A marketing résumé must reflect a business image. Accomplishments and potential should be described in terms of increased sales, reduced expenses, improved productivity, time saved, and advancement from one position to another. Stating accomplishments in terms of dollars and cents, percentages, increases and decreases, and profits and losses is reasonable and effective.

A teacher's résumé, however, only superficially resembles the typical business model. The focus, the emphasis, the vocabulary, and the overall message are different. Teachers should not attempt to follow the dictates of other occupations. The result will not strike the appropriate tone, nor will it focus on educational objectives. Teachers do not have a product, educational progress is not always and not necessarily measured in percentages, promotion is hardly an issue, and profitability is not the bottom line.

KNOW YOUR CULTURE

Caution: Each profession has its own culture, its own way of doing things, and to some extent its own language—certainly its own jargon. Do not use the language or techniques of another occupation to seek a teaching position. It is all too easy to adopt catchy terms and fashionable phrases, but educators must take care to stay within their own culture. Inappropriate use of popular buzz words can signal a lack of understanding of the profession or a misguided attempt to appear more knowledgeable or more qualified.

Even within the field of education, terminology is not uniform. Because each state has the responsibility of providing a system of public instruction for its citizens, the vocabulary and the definition of conditions, programs, and services is not uniform throughout the country. The terminology used in a particular state to describe a teaching specialization may be quite different from terms used even in neighboring states. Each state approves educational programs for its schools, determines requirements for certification, and issues licenses for teachers and administrators.

The problem is compounded by abbreviations and acronyms referring to teacher preparation programs, modes of instruction, and organizational systems. Although you may be familiar with several of these common abbreviations, you cannot assume that your reader will understand what is meant by IEP, CLP, BD, ED, LD, ESL, TOEFL, MR, MH, BH, ADD, AEA, CESA. Instead of using abbreviations, it is a good idea to spell out the terms, especially if you send your résumé to employers in other states.

SELF-PROMOTION IS GOOD PRACTICE

All successful job seekers have marketing plans. Teachers, too, must learn how to promote themselves, how to sell their skills and abilities to employers. Your challenge is to create a professionally appropriate résumé; a résumé that reflects your culture and that promotes you as a committed educator with experiences and abilities that are—if not unique—clearly consistent with current practices and procedures.

A résumé is an indispensable marketing tool.

EMPLOYERS EXPECT A RESUME

CLASSIFIED ADS

JOB OPENING

7th Grade Math Teacher

To apply, send

1) resume
2) cover letter
3) college placement file or three
   letters of recommendation

Apply to:

Personnel Office
Anytown Independent Schools
Box 804A, Anytown, State 11111-8041

COLLEGE JOB BULLETIN

Immediate Elementary Teaching Openings

Grades: 1) First

2) Fourth

3) Fifth/Sixth Combination

Contact: Personnel Office
Anytown Independent Schools
Box 804A, Anytown, State 11111-8041

In response to advertisements like these, many districts receive several hundred applications for each available position. Most schools ask candidates to furnish a résumé for initial screening purposes. From the application materials submitted, the employer creates a pool of qualified teachers for further consideration.

Hiring officials have a limited amount of time to make preliminary or first-round selections. Screening can be based solely on a quick scan of your resume and cover letter. It doesn't take long to make decisions —maybe thirty seconds, maybe even less. Surprising as it may seem, your résumé and your future can be relegated to a stack labeled *Yes*, *No*, or *Maybe* on the basis of a rapidly formed opinion.

Very few principals or superintendents would consider themselves experts in the area of constructing or critiquing a résumé. In the limited amount of time they can devote to the screening process, they make quick, hard decisions based on the following simple criteria:

★ Neat, fresh, legible, and error-free résumé

★ Clearly identified teaching field, skills, strengths

★ Effective language and correct grammar

★ Positive and promising professional image

Surviving this initial screening is critical but it is not particularly difficult. Avoiding the *No* bin or the wastebasket demands that your paper image be convincing, relevant, and positive.

4
WHAT GOES INTO A RESUME?

A résumé is built on facts: facts about you, your education, your background, your experiences. A good résumé presents the facts in a logical and meaningful sequence, telling potential employers who you are and what you have done, capturing their interest, and leading them to the desired conclusion.

Forcing the reader to solve a puzzle or unravel a mystery story deprives you of the opportunity to make a good first impression. You rarely have the luxury of a second chance.

THREE ESSENTIALS

Start with the basics. Be sure to include clear and direct information about these three essential items:

1. Identity

   Use your legal name, your full address, and your telephone number. Zip codes and area codes are important. This information seems obvious, but personnel departments and hiring officials frequently receive résumés lacking an address or telephone number.

2. Educational Background

   List academic degrees earned or in progress, major or field of study in which degrees were earned, and dates conferred or expected. Accuracy and honesty are critical.

3. Teaching Experience

   Any teaching experience (including full- or part-time professional experience, student teaching, practica, and internships) can be included on a résumé. Substantial professional experience can make it unnecessary to list early training experiences.

COMPILING RESUME FACTS

Take a few minutes to fill in the blanks with facts about yourself. Once you have listed these basics, you will have all the material you need to begin working on a draft of your résumé.

Identification

Name _____

Records under other names _____

Address _____

Telephone _____

It may be necessary to list both a temporary and a permanent address. It is permissible to indicate a termination date for the temporary address: for example, until June 1.

Other contact information can be included, such as:

FAX Number _____

E-mail Address _____

Education

Degree-granting Institutions: _____

Institution and Location _____

Attended from: _____ to: _____

Degree earned or in progress _____

Graduation date _____

Major: _____ Minor: _____

Area(s) of specialization: _____

Institution and Location _____

_____

Attended from: _____ to: _____

Degree earned or in progress _____

Graduation date _____

Major: _____ Minor: _____

Area(s) of specialization: _____

_____

Other Institutions Attended: _____

Institution and Location _____

Attended from: _____ to: _____

Major: _____ Minor: _____

Area(s) of specialization: _____

_____

Institution and Location _____

Attended from: _____ to: _____

Major: _____ Minor: _____

Area(s) of specialization: _____

_____

Teaching Experience

Information about internship experience or student teaching is essential for beginners and optional for teachers with professional experience. After more than a year or two of professional experience, information about preprofessional experience is generally included only if it indicates a different area of expertise or a significantly different grade level.

Position: _____

Employer: _____

Name and location of school or organization

Dates of Employment: _____ to: _____

Accomplishments: _____

_____

_____

Position: _____

Employer _____

Name and location of school or organization

Dates of Employment: _____ to: _____

Accomplishments: _____

_____

_____

BUT I HAVEN'T DONE ANYTHING SPECIAL...

Once you have completed the three basic sections, you might wonder what other information you need to incorporate. Procrastination can easily set in if you are convinced that you don't have anything but the basics to put into a résumé. Don't take this shortsighted view. You have a multitude of possibilities for additional sections. All teachers, beginners and experienced alike, have many special achievements, accomplishments, and significant experiences to relate.

Yes, everyone else completed student teaching or an internship. But no one had your particular experience. No one else achieved the same things, taught the same units, developed your unique style of teaching, or motivated the students in quite the same way. Very few people have taken exactly the same course work as you or had identical job or volunteer experiences.

It is a mistake to assume that your experiences are ordinary. Any hiring official will assume you have spent some time in a classroom in order to earn a teaching license. But no assumptions can be made about your achievements, your successes, your singular approach to good teaching. It is up to you to let your strengths be known.

A Special Note: Be careful not to overlook any unusual educational experiences. Special programs, summer institutes, foreign study tours, or a semester or year abroad can capture an employer's attention and make your resume stand out from the others in the pile. Most employers realize that educators who seek these supplemental experiences tend to be independent, intellectually curious, and committed to learning.

WHAT, NOT WHEN

Don't be unduly influenced by dates. What you have done is certainly more important than when you did it. For example, honors or other special recognitions rarely lose their impact. If you were inducted into Phi Beta Kappa twenty years ago, you can still consider this distinction a relevant item for your résumé. Being selected student body president, outstanding history student, or receiving the Volunteer of the Year award retains value long after the recognition was bestowed.

MORE FACTS...

In order to assemble additional facts for your résumé, the following checklist can help you recall previous experiences and activities. Quickly read through the list and check as many *Yes* responses as you can. Then come back and jot down the specifics. Don't worry about when it happened or the level of importance at this point. Don't worry about vocabulary and phrasing, either; just record the basic information. When you're ready to write a rough draft of your résumé, you can develop full-fledged entries based on your responses. Assigning priorities, refining the language, and polishing the individual sections will come later.

Yes No

❏ ❏ Language abilities

_____

_____

❏ ❏ Study or travel abroad

_____

_____

❏ ❏ Professional memberships

_____

_____

Yes No

❏ ❏ Committee leadership/membership

_____

_____

❏ ❏ Conference attendance/participation

_____

_____

❏ ❏ Volunteer activities/civic contributions

_____

_____

❏ ❏ Professional recognition

_____

_____

❏ ❏ Honors, awards, distinctions

_____

_____

❏ ❏ College activities

_____

_____

❏ ❏ Avocations and interests

_____

_____

❏ ❏ Exhibits, shows, publications

_____

_____

❏ ❏ Grants, special projects

_____

_____

❏ ❏ Teaching competencies

_____

_____

Yes No

❏ ❏ Extracurricular interests

_____

_____

❏ ❏ Recent courses of interest

_____

_____

❏ ❏ GPA (overall & major)

_____

_____

❏ ❏ Other work

_____

_____

❏ ❏ Other

_____

_____

DO I NEED A JOB OBJECTIVE?

Many people consider a job objective indispensable and expect to see it right at the top of a résumé. In some occupations, a job objective is both traditional and useful. A teacher, however, can convey a professional objective in a number of ways. You can express your interests, preferences, or priorities as *Teaching Competencies*, *Teaching Interests*, or *Special Skills*. Training in multiple teaching techniques, strategies, or methods and exposure to different teaching styles or settings can be communicated to a potential employer at a glance. Other sections of your résumé reinforce your objective and contribute to convincing the reader of your competence or expertise.

A useful job objective is clear, specific, and unencumbered with extraneous words. If you include an explicit statement of your job objective, restrict it to the nature of the position:

Head Basketball Coach

Journalism teacher and student newspaper advisor

Bilingual Kindergarten teacher

A note of caution: Too often, objectives look like this:

Objective: To obtain a position that is challenging, rewarding, and affords opportunity for personal growth and professional development.

Examine that statement. What does it say? And what message does it send? A close look reveals a mere series of words and phrases that are correct and proper and good and safe but have no real significance. They sound prefabricated if not pretentious. This calculated objective is too general to be of any use and is simply a waste of your space and the reader's time.

EVALUATING AND SELECTING

Look at all the things you have listed and select those entries that contribute to the image or picture you want to present to potential employers. Not everything is of equal value or importance, and you may decide that some items are no longer relevant and do not justify using space that could be taken by more current or more pertinent information.

Carefully and thoughtfully select items that emphasize your strongest assets and greatest interests.

ARRANGING YOUR INFORMATION

As you look over your list of facts and previous experiences, you will see that some of them can naturally be grouped together. Your résumé can have several sections representing different aspects of your educational background, interests, and experience. Each section can be assigned a descriptive heading to attract and to direct the reader's attention.

As you organize your material, the following list can help you select appropriate headings for the sections or divisions of your résumé.

SUGGESTED HEADINGS FOR YOUR RESUME

Degree(s)

Educational Background

Education

Educational Preparation

Academic Training

Study Abroad

Course Highlights

Courses of Interest

Academic Highlights

Course Concentration

Teaching Certificate(s)

Certificate(s)

License(s)

Licensure

Endorsements

Coaching Certification

Other Certification

Career Objective

Teaching Objective

Job Objective

Objective

Professional Objective

Position Desired

Teaching Strengths

Skills & Competencies

Teaching Competencies

Teaching Skills

Areas of Expertise

Areas of Knowledge

Special Skills

Special Talent

Teaching Experience

Professional Experience

Classroom Experience

Teaching Overview

Experience Highlights

Related Experiences

Student Teaching

Internship Experience

Practicum Experience

Practica

Field Experiences

Professional Seminars

Workshops Attended

Special Training

Inservice Training

Professional Activities

Current Activities

Exhibits

Shows

Publications

Presentations

Conference Participation

Seminar Presentations

Language Competencies

Language Ability

Languages

Travel Abroad

Travel

Overseas Travel

Foreign Experiences

International Experiences

Overseas Study

Professional Leadership

Professional Memberships

Affiliations

Professional Societies

Honorary Societies

College Distinctions

College Activities

Special Recognition

Academic Honors

Achievements

Honors & Distinctions

Awards

Scholarships

Extracurricular Interests

Coaching Skills

Coaching Interests

Club Advisor

Class Sponsor

Service

Committee Responsibilities

Committee Assignments

Departmental Service

Civic Contributions

Community Service	Part-time Work
Community Activities	Summer Work Experience
Civic Activities	Additional Experience
Community Involvement	Nonteaching Experience
Volunteer Activities	Military Service
Activities	Other Experiences
Leisure Activities	
Avocations	
Interests	References
	Credentials
Employment	Credential File
Other Work	Placement File

BREAKING THE ONE-PAGE RULE

Teachers often need more than one page to present a complete account of their qualifications, especially if they have professional experience in the classroom. Depending on the number of field-based experiences, even a beginner may find it necessary to use more than a single page.

By contrast, people in the business world usually try to restrict a résumé to a single page. A new graduate in finance or accounting would consider a second page unconventional and likely to create an unfavorable impression. Even a person with considerable experience might hesitate to expand to a second page. So powerful is the mystique surrounding a single-page résumé that even people who should not be bound by this rule are afraid to abandon it.

Quantity alone, however, is not the goal. There is such a thing as padding: Overzealous descriptions, annotations that pile detail upon insignificant detail, or long tedious lists of the most minute or routine activities can have the effect of trivializing every aspect of the résumé. Fit all relevant information on a single page if you can, but do not be afraid of offending the reader by expanding your resume beyond this arbitrary limit.

The goal of a résumé is to stimulate interest, not to overwhelm with detail. A résumé should be as long as it needs to be and as short as it can be.

Employers in education are more inclined to focus on the content than on the length. And they will be more favorably impressed with a résumé that is easy to read and pleasing to the eye.

WHAT GETS LEFT OUT?

Contrary to what you may have heard, it is not necessary to list every activity, include details of every experience, or account for every year. Your résumé is not your permanent record, your autobiography or a blueprint for your future.

Ambitions, dreams, speculations, long-range plans, and ultimate goals have their place in a job search. But they don't belong on your résumé.

BE CONSISTENT

Your résumé must agree with all information provided to an employer, but it does not have to duplicate other documents or contain every bit of data on your educational background. Employers will ask for your transcript, which will list all courses taken as well as grades earned and degrees conferred. Grade point average is not a standard entry on a teacher's résumé.

In the initial screening process, most hiring officials are not overly concerned with your grade point average. They scan your résumé to find evidence of your educational qualifications, your teaching experiences, and your demonstrated interest in working with children or youth. Unlike some employers in the business sector, school officials do not restrict serious consideration to candidates with a predetermined grade point average. Good grades are always an asset, never a detriment. But scholastic achievement is valued in combination with other special skills you can offer in the classroom. A high GPA does not guarantee that you will work successfully with children.

If your educational record gives the impression that you were a peripatetic student roving from campus to campus, you might want to list on your résumé only the institution that granted your degree. This is not a technique to deceive employers but a way to save valuable space to promote your teaching abilities. You are not obligated to list on your résumé every institution you have attended. The school district's application form will likely request a complete educational record, and your official transcripts will show attendance at all institutions from which you have transferred credits.

WHAT ABOUT REFERENCES?

If a job announcement specifically asks for names and addresses of references, you may choose to list them on your résumé or include their names in your application letter. Always get permission to list a person as a reference. You might give a copy of your résumé to anyone who agrees to serve as a reference. Your résumé can be a helpful resource when a recommendation is requested either in writing or by telephone.

The initial screening process usually does not require names and addresses of individual references and you need not waste space or time in providing them. Application forms almost always ask for references; there is no advantage to duplicating this information or providing names and addresses before they are requested.

CUTTING OUT THE DEAD WOOD

Experienced professionals should carefully review information about preprofessional training. Retaining outdated information can increase the length but not the impact of your résumé. Lists of practica or student teaching experiences that occurred several years ago are seldom worth the space they occupy. Moreover, they can divert attention from recent and more important professional development.

Activities dating back to high school or even college years may have little relevance to your current objective and are probably best omitted. There are always exceptions to this rule, however. For example, if you are qualified and interested in promoting yourself as a basketball coach but did not play on a college team, you could reach back to high school and briefly mention your participation in team sports. If you were an all-conference player or selected to an all-state team, the information will add some credibility to your potential as a coach. Similar examples could be given for yearbook sponsorship, cheerleading, debate, or any other school activity. If you are seeking a teaching position at a preparatory school or a parochial institution, it is probably a good idea to mention that you attended a similar school.

Your résumé is not an official document; you have the opportunity and the responsibility to determine the facts you want to present and the skills you want to emphasize.

DON'T WRITE YOUR AUTOBIOGRAPHY

During the selection process, all information requested by an employer should be job related. Hiring officials should not solicit information about marital or family status, disabilities, age, gender, race, ethnic background, religion, height, weight, or color of eyes and hair. Federal and state guidelines prohibit employers from gathering preemployment information of this sort. Obviously, this personal data is not job related. Because it does not affect your qualifications or your potential as an educator, there is no reason for you to volunteer this kind of information.

DON'T BELIEVE EVERYTHING YOU SEE...OR HEAR

Old books on library or resource center shelves (even some shiny new books at your local bookstore) contain examples and advice that should have been discarded years ago. These are the samples that helped your father or your Uncle Jack to land a job. In a prominent place, usually on page one immediately after the name and address, they listed information about their age, height, weight, marital status, wife's name if appropriate, and at least the number of children if not their names and ages. If the spouse or child had accomplished something significant, that might be included, too.

Because this type of résumé worked for them, Dad and Uncle Jack will probably advise you to put in the same sort of personal information. They may even suggest that you include a photograph of yourself, as they did, either by attaching a photo or actually having it printed on the page.

Do not listen to them.

Times are different now.

Laws have been enacted to prevent discrimination.

Including personal information is unsophisticated and reflects outmoded practices.

And never—ever—unless you are seeking work as a model or performer—send a photograph.

DON'T CLUTTER YOUR RESUME WITH NONESSENTIALS

Space on your résumé is valuable. Include only those items that can help you to promote your skills and abilities to potential employers. Don't squander space on irrelevant information. The employer will see it as a waste of time and interpret it as your inability to organize thoughts and data.

Your résumé does not need and should not contain these items:

1. *Title.* Reserve the most prominent location for your name. The reader will recognize a résumé without seeing the word "RESUME" as the first line of the first page. Keep the focus on you; a label is distracting and unnecessary.

2. *Philosophy Statement.* Your beliefs about teaching and the process of learning will very likely enter into the selection process, but do not use résumé space for this purpose. A statement of your personal educational philosophy may be requested as a part of the application form or as a question during an interview.

3. *Personal Statement.* Your résumé is not the proper vehicle for conveying biographical details about your upbringing or your early educational experiences. Similarly, how

you chose to pursue a teaching career, how you propose to conduct your classroom, or what you see yourself doing in the future are excellent topics for responses to open-ended questions on the application form or during the interview.

4. *Reason for Leaving Previous Position.* In a business resume, it is sometimes considered possible to make a positive statement of professional growth by citing reasons for leaving a position. One can show a progression, indicate greater opportunity for responsibility or higher earnings, or promotion to a new project or level. This practice does not work for teachers, and there is no reason to attempt to define your career path in business terms. Educators work in a different environment and a different culture, and they define their achievements with a different vocabulary. They can change positions, change responsibilities, and change job titles, but the system does not allow for promotion.

5. *Availability.* There is no need to state that you will be available for a position beginning immediately or at a specified future date. Hiring officials will assume that you can begin when needed. Although emergencies or unforeseen circumstances can require immediate hiring, starting dates are not usually open to negotiation. The selection process is geared to the academic year or to the beginning of a semester or trimester.

6. *Date Prepared.* Your résumé will be considered current so long as it reflects your latest experiences. Assigning a date, however, can make it appear outdated within a few months even though nothing has changed. Let your cover letter serve to indicate the date your résumé was submitted.

7. *Ability to Travel or Relocate.* This is another carry-over from the business world with little application to the field of education. Teachers might divide their responsibilities between schools in the same district, but overnight travel is simply not a factor for classroom teachers. A teacher may transfer from one building to another within a district, but because school districts are local entities, such transfer would rarely require changing one's residence.

8. *Salary.* Public school teachers generally do not have the opportunity to engage in individual negotiation for salary or benefits. A master contract governs placement on the salary scale, number of working days, holiday schedules, and conditions of employment. Salaries vary

from district to district, from state to state, and from region to region. Whether your previous salary exceeds or falls short of the possibilities in the district to which you are applying is of no consequence; therefore, salary history has no place on your résumé.

NO APOLOGIES, NO EXCUSES

If you have gaps in your education or in your employment record, a history of job-hopping, even if you have been fired, you can stress the positive aspects of your experience. Pay special attention to how you organize this material. For example, if you have frequently moved from job to job, you won't want to emphasize dates of employment. They can be placed at the end of the entry, or even buried in the middle. You are not being deceptive; you are emphasizing the experience rather than the chronology.

If health problems caused an interruption in your career, the gap might be apparent to a careful reader, but you should not attempt to explain it. Any illness serious enough to cause a job interruption tends to frighten prospective employers. Save your explanation for the interview when you have the opportunity to demonstrate that you are physically capable of discharging your duties and responsibilities.

Because you control the material presented in your résumé, you have the opportunity to present yourself in the best possible light. This does not mean you can be less than truthful. Every item on the résumé should work to your advantage: Stress the positives, avoid ambiguous or questionable entries, and weed out any item that could be construed as a negative. Accuracy and honesty are paramount, and misrepresentations, exaggerations, or actual lies are never acceptable.

As you begin to design your résumé, refer to the following model to remind you of what goes in and what gets left out.

HOME ADDRESS: (city, state, zip, phone)

TEACHING EXPERIENCE: (list student teaching, substituting, or full-time classroom positions; briefly outline responsibilities and accomplishments)

RELATED EXPERIENCE: (expand on projects or teaching-related activities; community contributions; volunteer service)

EMPLOYMENT: (list title of position, employer, location & dates; briefly describe duties)

ACTIVITIES & DISTINCTIONS: (leadership positions; academic honors; professional associations)

EDUCATION: (degrees held or in progress; continuing education classes; certificates; licenses)

INTERESTS: (academic; athletics; avocations)

REFERENCES: (list placement office or indicate available upon request)

- **NO** picture
- **NO** personal information (age, sex, race, religion, marital status)
- **NO** information about children, spouse, or significant other
- **NO** physical data (eye or hair color, weight, height)
- **NO** personal/philosophical statement
- **NO** date for résumé preparation or availability for employment
- **NO** salary information

ACTION
WORDS AND
PHRASES

The ability to write cohesive paragraphs employing a balanced variety of simple, complex, and compound sentences is a decided asset. This skill, however, is not required in writing a résumé. You can appropriately demonstrate your mastery of the language in your application letter and in other writing samples you may be asked to submit. At some point in the selection process, you will almost inevitably be asked to produce a short essay (often handwritten) describing your philosophy of education or your reasons for wanting to work in the district. Your résumé requires a different style of communication.

Active.

Quick.

Concise.

Convincing.

Action words and dynamic phrases create powerful impressions. Energize your activities, your skills, your accomplishments, with strong active language.

BE SELECTIVE

Avoid repetition; the impact of any word is diminished by too frequent use. Let's say you have developed five new instructional units that demonstrate your interest in several different curriculum areas. Your first draft might read like this:

Developed geography unit for third grade

Developed multi-grade unit on the solar system

Developed...

Obviously, this leads to monotony. Almost any approach would be better. An easy way to retain the impact of several similar activities without constant repetition might be:

Developed instructional units for various grade levels, including:

Looking at Latitude and Longitude (Grade 4)

Our Solar System (Grades 3–4)

Fractions are Fun (Grade 4)

Alphabets and Hieroglyphics (Grade 3)

Proper Nouns and Proper Caps (Grade 3)

USE ACTION WORDS

The following list of action words should help you get started. You can use some of these, or find other powerful verbs to create a dynamic picture of you and to suggest your potential.

Accomplish	Commended	Discover
Achieve	Communicate	Distinguish
Act	Compete	Distribute
Adapt	Compile	Diversify
Address	Complete	Draft
Administer	Compose	Edit
Advance	Compute	Educate
Advise	Conceptualize	Eliminate
Analyze	Conduct	Enable
Approve	Conserve	Encounter
Arbitrate	Consolidate	Encourage
Articulate	Consult	Enlist
Assemble	Contribute	Establish
Assess	Control	Evaluate
Assist	Coordinate	Examine
Attain	Correspond	Execute
Author	Counsel	Expand
Balance	Create	Explain
Budget	Critique	Facilitate
Build	Deliver	Familiarize
Catalog	Design	Find
Chair	Develop	Focus
Clarify	Devise	Formulate
Coach	Diagnose	Generate
Collect	Direct	Group

Guide	Operate	Revise
Identify	Organize	Revitalize
Illustrate	Originate	Rewarded
Implement	Overhaul	Schedule
Improve	Oversee	Screen
Incorporate	Participate	Select
Increase	Perform	Serve
Influence	Plan	Shape
Inform	Prepare	Skilled
Initiate	Present	Solidify
Innovate	Preside	Solve
Install	Process	Sponsor
Institute	Produce	Stimulate
Integrate	Program	Streamline
Interpret	Project	Strengthen
Interview	Promote	Study
Introduce	Provide	Summarize
Invent	Publicize	Supervise
Investigate	Publish	Systematize
Involve	Received	Teach
Launch	Recommend	Test
Lead	Record	Train
Lecture	Recruit	Translate
Maintain	Reduce	Travel
Manage	Refer	Trim
Mediate	Rehabilitate	Upgrade
Moderate	Repair	Utilize
Monitor	Represent	Validate
Motivate	Research	Venture
Network	Restore	Verify
Nominated	Restructure	Work
Observe	Reverse	Write
Obtain	Review	

Action words must be used accurately. Find a way to describe your role in any activity that neither overstates your case nor undervalues your achievement. If you chaired a committee, say so; just listing the name or function of the committee ignores your leadership role. On the other hand, if you were a member of a team that developed a new learning center, be careful about claiming all of the credit.

Discrepancies have a way of surfacing. Avoid placing yourself in a potentially awkward or embarrassing position.

SHORT PHRASES = EASY READING

One of the most effective methods of giving energy and life to your résumé is to make the writing flow easily and quickly. Complete sentences, however well constructed, cannot be read as quickly as fragments. Short phrases with strong verbs are easy to scan, conveying your message clearly and dynamically without verbal excess, redundant auxiliary verbs, or a clutter of personal pronouns. How long can anyone sustain interest when each sentence begins:

I was

I did

I have

I am

I made

I...

You get the idea. Sentence fragments allow you to skip over the repetitive personal pronoun and get directly to the important part, the activity or accomplishment, and to lead off each entry with a strong verb.

Suppose you found this on a résumé:

I have had the responsibility in April of each year for putting together the Washington School talent show which earned money for the general fund.

Look at the difference when an action phrase replaces a complete sentence:

Created and organized profitable annual school talent show

By combining your activities with strong action verbs, the phrases on your résumé might look something like this:

★ Utilized effective classroom management strategies

★ Planned, prepared, and organized materials for thematic units

★ Provided consistent enthusiasm and creativity in classroom activities

- ★ Individualized instruction for students at all levels and abilities
- ★ Facilitated the implementation of writing and reading strategies in ten elementary buildings
- ★ Developed a training packet for portfolio assessment
- ★ Instituted a new curriculum that included long-range plans to incorporate computer literacy into daily instruction

CREATE YOUR OWN ACTION PHRASES

On the lines below, write action phrases that describe your skills, abilities, and accomplishments.

_____

_____

_____

_____

_____

_____

_____

_____

_____

_____

_____

_____

_____

_____

_____

_____

_____

_____

Action words and phrases in your résumé will produce a significant bonus. When you begin to interview for positions, you will already have the habit of expressing yourself in language that makes you sound vital, energetic, and enthusiastic.

7

PRODUCTION GUIDELINES

Nothing about your résumé is more important than what it says about you, but potential employers may not pay attention to the content if the appearance does not create a good first impression. Imagine reading twenty résumés—or fifty, a hundred, a thousand, or more. Many hiring officials face exactly this task when they need to hire a teacher.

What can you do to make their job easier?

A hiring official responsible for reviewing application materials must look for quickly identifiable reasons to reject at least a portion of the applicants. Judging a résumé by its appearance requires comparatively little time or effort, and it is a standard and legitimate practice.

The old adage about not judging a book by its cover does not apply here. An unprofessional appearance makes a résumé easy to discard.

RESUME LAYOUT

The arrangement of material on the page is referred to as the layout. The position and alignment of the information in the various sections of your résumé can make a vital difference in how you are perceived. Don't rush this stage of your résumé development. The samples in this book use several different layouts. Experiment with the effect of different layouts on your material. An effective layout guides the reader through the information about your education and experience, directing attention to your strengths while allowing the reader to assess your résumé easily and quickly.

Although there are no prescribed layouts for résumés, three styles are commonly used because they are easily prepared and professional in appearance.

Layout #1
This résumé is set up with a full block style. Every heading begins at the left margin, creating a sharp, clean look. Locations, dates, and other details about professional background are uniformly indented from the left. The shorter line necessitated by this style makes it especially appropriate if you have a limited amount of material.

KEN B. EXAMPLE

221 College Street
Any City, State 12345
(101) 555-0009

OBJECTIVE: **Teacher: Russian Language (9-12)**

EDUCATION: The Ohio State University, Columbus, Ohio
   B.S. Degree - May 1995
      Major: Russian Language
      Teaching Certificate, May 1995
The Pushkin Institute, Moscow, Russia
   Exchange Program - September 1993 - June 1994
Middlebury College, Middlebury, Vermont
   Summer 1993 - Russian Language
Bryn Mawr College, Bryn Mawr, Pennsylvania
   Summer 1992 - Russian Language

STUDENT
TEACHING: **Russian Language**, Valley High School, Columbus, 1/95-5/95
Responsibilities:
• Prepared lesson plans and objectives for levels I-IV
• Reviewed curriculum resources and created new materials
• Attended departmental meetings and support groups
• Effectively used cooperative learning strategies
• Implemented higher order thinking skills
• Involved in International Club
• Organized and created grammar explanations, games, and activities

PRACTICUM
STUDENT: **English as a Second Language**, Art Middle School, Detroit, 9/94-1/95
Responsibilities:
• Assisted in all teaching responsibilities
• Provided tutorial services for students needing extra help
• Individually tutored new students

ACTIVITIES
& AWARDS: • Dean's List, 1990 - 1995
• Ohio Critical Language Program, accepted 1992
• Member, American Association of Slavic and Eastern
  European Languages
• Member, Dobro Slovo, Slavic Honor Society
• Buckeye Marching & Concert Band, 1990-1992
• President, Russian Circle, 1991

CREDENTIALS
ON FILE: Teacher Career Center
Any City, State 12345 (101) 555-0008

Layout #2

This résumé uses centered section headings, and full margins for each entry. The wider line readily accommodates a larger volume of information. With appropriate indentation to allow for ample white space, the résumé can handle a longer text without resorting to dense blocks of print. It can also handle a shorter text if several indentations are made within entries or additional space separates each section.

ANNE EXAMPLE
221 College Street
Any City, State 12345
(101) 555-1111

DEGREES
M.A. Special Education, Texas Woman's University, Denton, Texas June 1992
   Thesis: Community Mobility of Emotionally Disturbed Teenagers in Group Home Settings
   Adviser: Dr. Will B. Prof, Department Chair
B.A. Special Education Emphasis: Behavior Disorders May 1984

CLASSROOM EXPERIENCE
Special Education Teacher, grades 10 - 12, Special Services Alternative Center, Dallas, Texas, August 1993 - present. Case manager for emotionally and behaviorally disturbed students removed from local high school programs. Responsibilities include interfacing with outside referral agencies on behalf of students, coordinating the instructional programs, developing appropriate Individual Education Plans, and designing and monitoring specialized behavior management programs.

Special Education Teacher, grades 7 & 8, Connally Independent School District, Waco, Texas, 1990 - 1992. Self-contained with integration classroom for emotionally disturbed students. Major teaching responsibilities included reading, mathematics, and social studies. Implemented initial stages of the special education immersion program placing students in regular academic classrooms.

Special Education Teacher, grades 5 - 12, North Texas Residential Care Center, Dallas, Texas, 1986 - 1990. Semi-residential placement center for emotionally disturbed students ages 10 to 18. Teaching responsibilities included all curricular areas. Assisted psychologist in assessment of students with behavioral or emotional problems.

UNIVERSITY ASSISTANTSHIP
Supervisor of Student Teachers, Texas Woman's University, Denton, Texas, 1992 - 1993.
Supervised undergraduate special education student teachers in three school districts. Provided guidance to students regarding their instructional techniques and overall classroom performances during semester-long internship experience.

RELATED WORK EXPERIENCE
Systems Unlimited Inc., Dallas, Texas, 1984 - 1986
   Teacher for Summer Program, 1984 - 1986
   Planned activities for 12 to 16-year-old behavior disorder students.
   Family and Child Trainer, 1985 - 1986
   Provided 24-hour care for three severe/profound girls ages four to six.
   Direct Care Staff, 1984 - 1985
   Charged with the complete care of five severe/profound disabled teenagers
   in a group home setting.

PRESENTATIONS
"Evaluation of Video Feedback as a Training Procedure for BD Students." Poster presentation
   at the Convention for the Association for Behavior Analysis, Phoenix, Arizona, April 1994.
"Alternative Settings for Success." Presentation at the Texas Special Education Conference,
   San Antonio, Texas, November 1993.
"Community Mobility and Special Populations." Breakout session facilitator, Special Education
   Regional Convention, Corpus Christi, Texas, May 1992.

References provided upon request.

Layout #3

This résumé style positions the section headings at the left margin, allowing a wide line for entries. Because the entire page can be used, it is a good choice if you need to include extensive descriptions or a number of different experiences. Vertical spacing and indenting from both the left and right margins can help to achieve a balance between text and white space.

IMA MODEL
221 College Street
Any City, State 12345
(101) 555-0009

EDUCATION

Secondary English - Licensure Program, Urban Teacher Development Project
Paterson Public Schools, Paterson, New Jersey, 1994-1995
The Urban Teacher Development Project awards full scholarships for study and internship opportunities leading to a professional teaching license. The Project is directed by the Paterson Public Schools in collaboration with faculty from teacher preparation institutions throughout the state who teach courses and collaborate with practitioners in the schools to supervise student teaching or internship experiences.

B.A. - Majors in English and Psychology
Glassboro State College, Glassboro, New Jersey, 1988-1992

TEACHING EXPERIENCE

Internship:
Eastside High School, Paterson, New Jersey, January-June, 1995
Taught Contemporary Writing and Basic English
Created individual reading plans for each student in Contemporary Writing, an elective course for students in grades 11 and 12 reading at or near grade level. Readings included fiction, essays, and poetry. Emphasized critical reading skills, demonstrated in oral and written responses to readings. In Basic English, required for grade 10, developed units on vocabulary building and expository writing.

Practicum Experience
Eastside and John F. Kennedy High Schools, Paterson, New Jersey, November-December, 1994
Observed classes taught by mentors, assisted with presentation of units for individual and group projects in spelling and punctuation. Worked with students individually and in small groups to improve written and oral communication.

RELATED EXPERIENCE

Counselor, Passaic County Family Court, Paterson, New Jersey, 1992-1993
Assisted victims of domestic violence in petition room filing for Orders of Protection. Provided advocacy, crisis intervention, and short-term counseling to victims of domestic violence. Provided clients with an orientation to Family Court and escorted clients to court as required. Assisted clients with direct services, such as shelters, relocation, transportation, public assistance, and referrals for long-term assistance.

Volunteer, Crisis Intervention Center, Glassboro, New Jersey, 1990-1992

REFERENCES

Dr. Sue Pervisor	Mr. Abel Mentor	Dr. E. Val Waite
Paterson Public Schools	Eastside High School	Glassboro State College
Paterson, New Jersey 07509	Paterson, New Jersey 07509	Glassboro, New Jersey 08028
(101) 555-0100	(101) 555-0101	(101) 555-0102

WHITE SPACE

A judicious use of white space creates a layout that is both attractive and easy to read. White space makes your résumé far more inviting than a cramped, dense block of text bristling with dates and locations. Ample margins, extra spaces between sections, indentation, and the use of columns can all contribute to an airy and accessible effect.

FONTS OR PRINT SIZES

Variable sizes of print can make your résumé interesting and reader friendly as well as allow you to emphasize section headings, important assignments, or specific preparations. Scalable fonts available with many personal computers make it possible to design an eye-catching résumé that subtly draws the reader's attention to the points you wish to emphasize.

Italic print can be used for emphasis, or simply for variety. Similarly, underlining, **boldface**, and CAPITAL LETTERS can be useful techniques. Overuse of any of these accent techniques will diminish their effect.

Don't get carried away with variety for variety's sake. Efficient communication depends on the twin goals of clarity and legibility. Unusual fonts such as "olde Englishe" or script or shadowed letters or gothic characteristics can be distracting, and even irritating. Keep your choices few, simple, and meaningful.

Hints:

★ Nothing should be larger than your name

★ Section headings should be of uniform size

★ Annotations can appear less formidable and take up less of your valuable space if they use a slightly smaller font.

★ Overuse of large print wastes space, is difficult to scan, and may look like an attempt to stretch limited information.

GRAPHICS

Design your resume to direct the reader's attention to your strong points. Simple graphic techniques can achieve attractive and professional results. For example, a small bullet or other symbol (● ○ ■ ❑ ♦ ★) can draw attention to a special item, or unify similar entries:

○ Elected student body president

○ Nominated for Teacher of the Year

○ Selected Rhodes Scholar regional finalist

Section headings can be accented with straight lines, making the divisions of your résumé more prominent.

Your name and address can be highlighted by creating a box or by combining one or more graphics features to create a personalized heading.

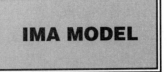

OTHER GRAPHICS

An art teacher could appropriately use an original design or logo. Designs, figures, clip art, or drawings are possible graphic enhancements for any résumé. Used very sparingly, a simple graphic can be effective and attractive. On the other hand, intricate patterns, cute figures, or large, bold designs appear gimmicky and draw attention away from the message of the résumé.

DOES THE LAYOUT WORK FOR YOU?

Check these features to enhance your résumé's appearance. Which features could improve the visual impact and the communication ability of your résumé?

- ✓ Ample margins
- ✓ White space
- ✓ Capital letters
- ✓ Bold type
- ✓ Underlining
- ✓ Italics
- ✓ Highlighting
- ✓ Accents, such as:

THE FINAL PRODUCT

As you approach the final stages of résumé preparation, you must become not only a writer but an editor. If you were writing for publication, you would have the luxury of working with an editor who could read your work with a clear and objective eye. The editor would catch inaccuracies and inconsistencies. Problems arising from ambiguities, extraneous language, and faulty organization would be spotted and resolved.

These editorial functions must be performed before your résumé is ready for production. If you are persuasive enough, you might talk someone else into editing your résumé for you. With or without assistance, you have ultimate responsibility for the final product. No one is in a better position to make editorial decisions about the relevance of each entry, the importance of individual word selection, and the effect created by the arrangement of the material.

Perhaps the most difficult aspect of editing your own material is deciding what to cut out. Everything you have put into your draft is there because it seems relevant. As a beginning teacher or a veteran with years of experience, you have to challenge the significance of each item, to question whether its contribution justifies the space it requires. Sometimes you can compromise; sometimes you simply have to be ruthless in your actions.

After you have drafted, revised, and edited your résumé, there is one more step before you are ready to produce the genuine article. That important step is proofreading.

Never Neglect or Underestimate the Importance
of Proofreading

One simple mistake can be disastrous. Take the time to check each word for spelling and each entry for accuracy, grammar, and punctuation. Make full use of a computer's spell-checker if you can, but don't rely on it completely. It won't recognize a misplaced or misused word if it is spelled correctly.

You have the ultimate responsibility for the document, but you probably will not be the best proofreader. After you have written, rewritten, chopped, added, cut and pasted, thrown it away and started over, you will very likely see what you expect to see. Get help from friends, colleagues, roommates, instructors—anyone who is willing and reasonably knowledgeable—even Uncle Jack. Make any necessary changes or corrections, then move into the production stage.

METHODS OF PRODUCTION

Computers

The availability of campus computer systems and of personal computers has made dramatic changes in the way most résumés are produced. Tailoring a résumé to meet the requirements of a specific job, rearranging categories to highlight particularly appropriate skills or experiences, or simply updating and changing an address is quickly and easily accomplished. Word processing or desktop publishing allows you to design a format that fits your needs and to select layout features to enhance your message. Any printer can give you a draft version so you can begin to see how your résumé will look. A good printer can give you a sophisticated finished copy that is ready to represent you as a professional.

Print Quality. Only a clear, sharp image is acceptable. Most dot matrix printers are incapable of producing a satisfactory final copy. If you have access to a letter-quality printer, you can produce copies as you need them. If your printer cannot provide the quality you desire, or if you do not have access to a printer, many print shops can process your résumé from your diskette, either in the form you have delivered or adding desktop publishing features.

Typewriter

Typewritten resumes remain a viable option, though you need not attempt to type an original for each submission. Photographic reproduction from a perfectly typed original is easy and economical. Take your original to a copy shop—the quality will be much better than self-service copiers, and you can choose the weight, finish, and color of paper you prefer.

Typeset

Though it has been nearly eclipsed by the advent of personal computers, professional typesetting remains an option because it offers a great variety of typefaces and sizes, and it requires comparatively little effort from the writer. A print specialist can prepare your résumé from your handwritten notes, design a layout, and offer suggestions to make your résumé attractive and effective. Be sure that the information you furnish to the printer is perfect: Check your spelling, dates, and grammar, and carefully check the proof copy before authorizing production.

No Hand Work

Professional papers are not handwritten. You may have the most sophisticated handwriting, you may print beautifully, or you may even be a master of calligraphy, but your résumé is not the place to demonstrate these abilities. It is also unprofessional and unadvisable to make handwritten corrections, additions, or updates to a conventionally produced résumé.

MULTIPLE PAGES

If your résumé consists of more than one page, each page after the first should be numbered. Your name should appear on every page. Do not fasten the pages together with staples or clips and never print on both sides of the page.

Presentations on 11 × 17 inch paper, folded in half to create a brochure effect, can be attractive, but they are difficult to scan or to copy Because they require a minimum of two full pages of text, they are unsuitable for nearly all beginning teachers, who may attempt to fill a brochure with large fonts, extra spacing, or extraneous descriptions. Even for experienced professionals, the brochure offers no clear advantage.

PAPER

The paper you select for your résumé contributes to your professional image. It does not have to be the most expensive stock available, but it should be at least twenty-pound bond. Standard size for a professional resume is 8 1/2 × 11 inches. Larger or smaller paper is usually more of a nuisance than an asset; it doesn't stack or file properly, and it cannot be copied as readily.

The exact weight or texture of the paper you select is a matter of personal taste, but anything truly unusual should be avoided. Similarly, the use of colored stock is a legitimate option. Soft tints in neutral colors are acceptable and can be attractive. Bright colors will, indeed, attract attention, but perhaps not the kind of attention you want to receive. Plain white paper is always a viable option for creating a crisp, professional image.

Using the same paper for your correspondence with employers is a good idea. Matching envelopes are a nice added touch, though the envelope is often discarded immediately upon opening.

YOUR RESUME REPRESENTS YOU

Anything less than perfection will detract from your overall impression. Evidence of carelessness in producing or handling the document, any smudge, stain, dog-eared corner, or unnecessary crease or fold, is grounds for immediate rejection.

A good-looking résumé will get you noticed; you get only one chance to make a good impression.

Avoid submitting a résumé that does not represent your best interests. Any of the following flaws could be fatal to your chances.

FATAL RESUME FLAWS

- Lack of focus or direction
- Long, rambling sentences
- Crowded, cramped appearance
- Use of personal pronoun
- Dense blocks of narrative
- Poor print quality (light, faded)
- Strange or inappropriate graphics
- Inconsistent format
- Reused or recycled appearance
- Typographical errors or misspellings
- Smudges, stains, wrinkles
- Handwritten changes or corrections
- Unusual or careless folding

CUSTOMIZING YOUR RESUME

A résumé should be designed to accomplish a specific purpose; in other words, your résumé must fit the job. Tailoring a résumé for specific jobs can be easily accomplished. By rearranging categories, highlighting the most relevant experiences or qualifications, adding or deleting details, you can target a specific job. Personal computers make this a simple task.

For example, if you are certified to teach social studies, you will probably start with a résumé that presents your qualifications as a generalist. As opportunities arise, modifications can be made to reflect your preparation in such specific areas as American history, government, world history, or international affairs.

A music teacher, for example, may be licensed to work with students from kindergarten through twelfth grade in general and vocal music. One résumé could emphasize preparation and experience for working with high school choral groups; another version could concentrate on a general music program for elementary students.

A RESUME IS NOT AN ALL-PURPOSE DOCUMENT

Your employment résumé addresses skills, strengths, competencies, extracurricular interests, and educational background. If you are seeking two distinctly different kinds of positions, such as classroom teacher and school principal, you need to prepare more than one résumé. Obviously, these positions have different responsibilities; they require different preparations and different skills. A teaching résumé, however well prepared, will send the wrong message in an administrative search: It could imply that you are insufficiently aware of the differences between teaching and administration, that you have not given enough thought to changing jobs, or that you are simply a poor communicator.

RESUMES FOR ADMINISTRATORS

Résumés for educators in administrative or supervisory roles focus on competencies and experiences directly related to immediate objectives. A teacher seeking an entry-level administrative position must demonstrate successful teaching experience as well as leadership capabilities and responsibilities assumed in school or community projects.

Service or leadership at the department, building, or district level illustrates interest, commitment, and involvement.

In addition to an employment history, experienced administrators should provide evidence of current and continuing development. Membership in professional associations is expected; presentations, recognitions, or positions of responsibility at the local, regional, or national level should be highlighted.

If you are a veteran administrator, a complete list of your activities and responsibilities over the years could produce a document running to several single-spaced pages. For maximum impact, priorities must be assigned in order to trim your résumé to a manageable size. Editing —selecting, summarizing, and condensing your career experiences and achievements into an effective promotional package—could be your most difficult task.

Your résumé will be carefully reviewed, often by many different people involved in the selection process, from school board officials to community representatives. Acronyms, abbreviations, technical terminology, and currently fashionable catchwords should be used very sparingly or avoided. The content of your résumé must be comprehensible to people who are not trained educators, yet sufficiently detailed to be meaningful to practicing professionals.

Accuracy is paramount; any error, inconsistency, or misrepresentation will prove damaging if not fatal. An attractive, purposeful résumé will enhance your image as a dynamic, knowledgeable leader.

RESUMES FOR OVERSEAS TEACHING

A specialized résumé will be essential if you are seeking a teaching position in another country. Headmasters from international schools are looking for people who are flexible, adaptable, and independent. A résumé that reflects these essential qualities and portrays you as a versatile teacher who can contribute to several different areas of school life will immediately catch the international employer's attention.

There are a few adjustments you will need to make on a résumé that is designed solely for overseas teaching opportunities. In addition to presenting your credentials as a teacher, the following items can be genuine assets:

- Foreign Language Ability
  In American-sponsored international schools, the language of instruction will be English. You need not be fluent in the language of the host country to be considered for employment. Knowledge of any foreign language, however, will contribute to your ability to learn the language of your new community and will make for an easier transition.

- International Experience
  Previous experience of living and/or studying in another country will be viewed positively by prospective employers. If you spent a summer, a semester, or an academic year

abroad, be sure to include all relevant information. Exchange students who have the advantage of living with a host family may have an easier adjustment to living in a new setting.

- Travel

    Experienced travelers are more likely to adjust quickly to a new setting. Even a limited exposure to different cultures, new surroundings, and unfamiliar customs, will usually lessen the severity and shorten the duration of the inevitable culture shock.

- Related Interests

    A demonstrated commitment to learning about other cultures and a concern for international affairs can be displayed on your résumé by stating membership in various kinds of international clubs or associations, volunteer service as a guide, language partner, or "friend" to foreign students, or even by elective courses in relevant ethnic, cultural, or area studies.

- Other Interests

    Leisure time can pose problems for people who depend on activities or resources not universally available. Avocations (photography, philately, sketching, reading, needlework, writing, hiking, and sightseeing) that can be pursued independently and without group or family support provide yet another indication of probable success in adjusting to a strange environment.

Unlike stateside hiring officials, directors of international schools may have a genuine need to be aware of your marital status and number of dependents. In some locations, housing suitable for families is simply not available. Only single teachers or a teaching couple with no dependent children can be considered for employment. The extreme difficulty or sheer impossibility of obtaining a work permit for a non-teaching spouse can also make it necessary for employers to hire only teaching couples or single teachers.

A special section of your résumé should be devoted to personal information including citizenship, marital status, and number of dependents who would accompany you. It is not necessary to include vital statistics (age, height, weight, religion, or ethnic identity). See résumés in the International Education section.

RESUMES FOR NONCERTIFIED TEACHERS

The traditional route to a career in education is through a teacher preparation program leading to licensure or certification. Even without a teaching license, it is possible to explore employment opportunities in schools and other settings.

Independent Schools

Some states do not require state certification for teachers in nonpublic or independent schools, a classification that can include preparatory schools, boarding schools, and parochial schools. Independent schools may offer internship or teaching fellowship opportunities for first-year teachers. Typically, a fellowship provides a stipend rather than a full salary.

Alternative Routes to Certification

A number of states have implemented alternative routes to certification. Provisional or substandard certificates can be issued for college graduates who lack required course work and practicum experience. Some states issue provisional certificates only in areas where there is a severe shortage of licensed teachers. In other states, alternative routes to certification may be possible in any teaching field.

English Language Instruction

Language centers around the world employ native speakers as instructors of conversational English. Major corporations and educational institutions in South America, Africa, Asia, and Eastern Europe hire college graduates interested in living and teaching in a different environment and culture. Teaching experience and certification are not required. Although advertisements frequently refer to ESL, TOEFL, or TESOL, teaching positions may not require specific training in English or linguistics.

Preschools

Preschool and daycare centers afford opportunities for college students and for college graduates who are interested in working with young children. Teaching certificates are not typically required, although some states license head teachers or directors of daycare centers.

RESUME TIPS

Information about preprofessional activities such as student teaching or practicum experiences, is an important résumé section for licensed teachers. Noncertified teachers must concentrate on other experiences that highlight related background, appropriate skills, and demonstrated abilities.

Special attention must be given to selecting, assigning priorities to, and arranging résumé items. The same person could conceivably prepare a résumé for teaching either in a preschool or a college preparatory school. Much of the information would be the same; however, sections of the résumé could be modified to emphasize different skills and experiences.

Experience with appropriate age groups

Volunteer activities

Personal attributes

Relevant course work

Special skills

Cultural awareness

Travel

Language skills

Involvement/Activism/Leadership

RESUMES FOR OTHER PURPOSES

Perhaps the most widely recognized use of a résumé is in the employment process, but educators will find many other situations in which a résumé can be a useful tool:

○ Evaluations/performance reviews

○ Grant proposals

○ Applications for special honors, awards

○ Conference presentations

○ Candidacy for election to office in a professional association

○ Background material for person who introduces or promotes speeches, talks

A résumé used for general introductions presents experiences, leadership roles, recognitions, and other accomplishments selected and arranged for their relevance. For example, if you are to present a paper or a talk at a professional conference, you might be asked to provide background information to the person who will introduce you. You would prepare a different résumé for the person who will introduce your address to a local service club. See examples on pages 100 and 144.

Similarly, you might find it necessary to prepare a résumé for a performance review or evaluation, to accompany a grant application, or to provide information when you are a candidate for office in a professional association. A résumé can also be helpful in support of your nomination or application for an award. Each of these occasions requires a customized résumé that could be quite different from the résumé sent to a potential employer. The content, the arrangement, and the emphasis must be directed toward the proper goal.

Note: Shortcuts won't work. Take time to prepare different versions. Your résumé must be appropriate for the purpose.

10

EFFECTIVE COVER LETTERS

Even the greatest soloists usually require an accompanist. Your best résumé, too, will need a companion piece—usually called a cover letter.

Writing a good basic cover letter is much easier than preparing a résumé. You have fewer choices to worry about; there are simple conventions for standard business letters, and you should follow them.

- Use standard 8½ × 11 stationery, preferably the same paper stock you have chosen for your résumé.
- Type (or, with a word processor, print) on one side of the page only.
- Your mailing address and the date should appear at the top of the page.
- Type the name of the person and institution three spaces below the date and flush with the left margin.
- The body of the letter should be single-spaced, with double spacing between paragraphs.
- Paragraphs may begin at the left margin or five spaces to the right.
- Type the complimentary close two spaces below the last line of the letter.
- Type your name four spaces below the complimentary close to allow room for your signature.

BEYOND THE MECHANICS—OR, WHAT DO I WRITE?

Start at the beginning. You cannot go wrong by clearly stating the purpose of your letter in your opening sentence—or at least in the first paragraph.

Once the opening lines are out of the way, go on to the main idea. In a letter of application for employment, this means pointing out specific qualifications and experiences directly related to the available position. This middle section of your letter can also provide information about supporting documents such as references or transcripts.

A letter of application should always include some reference to the next step in the process—the interview. You may request an appointment directly or use a slightly more subtle phrase such as, "I am very interested in this position and look forward to discussing it with you," but let the reader know that you want to arrange an interview.

COMMUNICATION IS THE GOAL

The ability to write clear, elegant prose is certainly an asset, but you don't have to be a great writer to produce a good letter. And you don't have to get writer's block when you sit down to compose a cover letter.

Complete sentences grouped in cohesive paragraphs are all that is required. Pay careful attention to spelling, grammar, and punctuation. Keep your language professional but simple; resist any temptation to inflate your vocabulary in order to sound more intellectual or knowledgeable. No literary prizes are at stake; all you need to do is convey your message clearly and correctly.

SAMPLE COVER LETTER

221 College Street
Any City, State 12345
March 26, 1995

Dr. A. J. Stephens
Superintendent
Independent School District #6-A
City, State 12321

Dear Dr. Stephens:

Please consider me as an applicant for the Junior High
language arts position on your staff. I learned of this
vacancy from my college placement office at Southern State
College, where I will earn my bachelor's degree in May of
this year with a major in English education and a minor in
journalism.

As the enclosed résumé indicates, I am completing a full
semester as a student teacher in Adams Middle School. In
addition to my classroom experience, I have volunteered to
assist with the school's newspaper. Because of my interest
in student publications, I am particularly interested in the
position in your district, which includes responsibilities
for advising the student magazine.

As your vacancy notice instructs, I have arranged to have
references and a copy of my transcript forwarded to you. I
look forward to receiving your application materials and to
arranging an interview at your convenience.

Sincerely,

Anne Example

Enclosure

PART TWO

SAMPLE RESUMES

11

MAKING THE BEST USE OF THESE SAMPLES

If you did nothing more than page through the following samples, find the one that most closely matches your teaching area, and plug in your own information, you'd have an acceptable résumé. It might even look as good as most of the others in the stack on the employer's desk.

But it wouldn't be the best résumé you could create. You don't have to settle for just a satisfactory appearance. Your résumé can do more than merely convey information to someone else; it can help you identify and concentrate on your particular strengths and interests, and organize your thoughts in preparation for interviews.

Take the time to read Part I of this book so you will understand how to capitalize on your strengths and abilities and how to convey these strengths and abilities to potential employers. Once you have read the introductory material, you will see how the samples work. You will understand how to highlight a special skill, how to empha-size a particular experience, and how to minimize events or circum-stances that could be perceived as liabilities.

The sample résumés represent a wide variety of teaching interests, fields, specializations, and experiences. It would be natural to start with the one that seems to be the closest match. Before you adopt this résumé as your model, however, look at several others. You may find one in a different teaching field that is better suited to your particular situation.

Don't hesitate to combine elements of different samples. You might choose the layout from one, the category headings from another (with your own modifications), the font or typeface from a third, a graphic from yet another. You can borrow, incorporate, or adapt from any num-ber of samples to create your personal résumé.

Add your own touches as well. The final product will represent you as a distinctive individual:

- an educator with an awareness of teaching capabilities and special strengths;

- an educator with recognized talents and accomplishments; and

- an educator who demonstrates personal commitment and pro-fessional purpose.

12

BEGINNING TEACHERS

ROSE LARA

221 College Street
Any City, State 12345
(101) 555-0009

TEACHING OBJECTIVE
  Bilingual Kindergarten Teacher

STRENGTHS
  Multicultural teaching experience
  Fluent in Spanish
  Trained in early childhood developmental philosophy
  Understand the educational needs of at-risk students

TEACHING EXPERIENCE
  Natchitoches Preschool Center, Natchitoches, Louisiana, Spring 1995
    Kindergarten & Prekindergarten Intern

  Responsibilities in the five-month internship include:
  - Develop and conduct classroom lessons in both Spanish and English
  - Reinforce material by involving non-English speaking parents in the classroom and school activities
  - Write and implement IEP's for each student and review with parents in school or home-based conferences
  - Work extensively with individual students in beginning reading program
  - Use cultural activities, songs, and materials to enhance learning and self-esteem

CLASSROOM EXPERIENCES
  Cloutierville Elementary School, Cloutierville, Louisiana, Fall 1994
    Transitional First Grade Practicum

  Goldonna Elementary School, Goldonna, Louisiana, Summer 1993
    First Grade Reading Recovery Program Observation

  North Natchitoches Elementary School, Natchitoches, Louisiana, Spring 1992
    Bilingual Kindergarten Practicum

COLLEGE ACTIVITIES
  Member, Gamma Phi Beta Sorority - Newsletter Editor, Pledge Director, Treasurer
  Player/coach, Intramural Basketball; volunteer referee and time keeper
  Board Member, Student Activities Council
  Co-chair, Dragon Boat Festival

COMMUNITY SERVICE
  Habitat for Humanity Volunteer, St. Tammany and Lafourche Parishes, Louisiana
  Spring breaks & summers, present. Work with student and adult volunteers from various parts of the country to rebuild homes for families in need.

EDUCATIONAL BACKGROUND
  Northwestern State University, Natchitoches, Louisiana
  Bachelor of Arts Degree, May 1994 Major: Early Childhood; Minor: ESL

CREDENTIALS
  Education Placement Office, Any City, State 12345
  Telephone: (101) 555-0008   FAX: (101) 555-0089

ANNA HANSEN

221 College Street
Any City, State 12345
(101) 555-0009

OBJECTIVE

Teacher: Early Childhood Education
Preschool Education

EDUCATION

University of Utah, Salt Lake City, Utah
B.A. Degree - May, 1995
Major: Early Childhood Education
Area of Specialization: Psychology

COURSE HIGHLIGHTS

Educational Psychology   Early Childhood Teaching
Language and Society   Multicultural-Bilingual Education
Child Development   Spanish I-IV

STUDENT TEACHING

Early Childhood Center, Head Start Center, Pioneer, Utah, 9/94-12/94

Responsibilities:
• Instructed a diverse student population including ESL students
• Taught individualized math using manipulatives
• Organized and created learning centers and bulletin boards
• Used cooperative learning strategies
• Introduced computer use in learning centers
• Provided students with individualized attention
• Created flannel board stories to enhance learning
• Kept concise records of students' progress
• Worked productively with staff, students, and parents

Pre-Kindergarten, Jensen Elementary, Salt Lake City, Utah, 1/95-4/95

Responsibilities:
• Developed learning stations in reading and science
• Taught reading to a small group of beginning readers
• Designed and maintained progress charts
• Worked closely with three disabled children
• Communicated with parents on a regular basis
• Attended child study team meetings and staffing for
  learning disabled

RELATED ACTIVITIES

Hospital tutor, University of Utah Medical Center, summer, 1991-1993
HACAP volunteer, Hooper Community Center, Hooper, Utah, 1989-1991
Swim instructor, Civic Center, Grantsville, Utah, 1989-1991
Member, National Association for Young Children

CREDENTIALS

Career Planning & Placement
Any City, State 12345 Telephone: (101) 555-0008

DEREK MARKS

PRESENT ADDRESS
221 College Street
Any City, State 12345
(101) 555-0009

PERMANENT ADDRESS
30 Royal Avenue
Mytown, State, 23456
(909) 333-0003

TEACHING INTERESTS
Primary Grades (K-3)

COACHING INTERESTS
Soccer - all levels
Assist in basketball, track
Coaching authorization - State of Idaho

ACADEMIC BACKGROUND
Idaho State University, Pocatello, Idaho
B.A. Degree, July, 1994
Major: Elementary Education; Specialization in Early Childhood
Dean's List, Idaho State University
School of Education tuition scholarship

STUDENT TEACHING EXPERIENCE
First Grade, Towers Elementary, Boise, Idaho   *3/94 to 5/94*
Kindergarten, Briggs Elementary, Boise, Idaho   *1/94 to 3/94*
Early Childhood Center, Springs, Idaho   *Summer 1993*

Responsibilities during the above teaching positions included:
- Planning and organizing materials for thematic units
- Use of systematic lesson planning emphasizing long and short term goals and assessment
- Implementation of positive classroom management strategies
- Motivation of students through an active learning environment
- Extensive utilization of manipulatives in math and science
- Communication with parents through a weekly newsletter

PRACTICA EXPERIENCE
Kindergarten, Hoover Elementary, Kuna, Idaho, Spring '93
Early Childhood Program, Hope Elementary, Idaho Falls, Summer '92
HACAP Head Start Community Center, Idaho Falls, Spring '92
Third Grade, Lakeview Elementary, Santa, Idaho, Fall '90

RELATED ACTIVITIES
Idaho Association for the Education of Young Children
Child Abuse Identification and Reporting Training
American Heart Association CPR Certification

ATHLETIC EXPERIENCES
All-Conference Soccer Selection   Soccer Coach, under 10 co-ed
Coach, Summer Soccer Camps   MVP Soccer Award
Medallion Award, Athletic Department   Certified soccer referee

WORK EXPERIENCE
Soccer Connection, clerk, 10/90 to 12/91
Athletic Club, server, 5/92 to present

Credentials at Career Planning & Placement
Any City, State 12345 (101) 555-0008 FAX: (101) 555-0089

RACHEL BRAVEHEART
221 College Street
Any City, State 12345
(101) 555-1111

DEGREES
B.A. Elementary Education, University of Nebraska - Lincoln   June 1995
Area of Specialization: Language Arts   Minor: Native American Studies
A.A. Liberal Arts, Nebraska Indian Community College, Winnebago, Nebraska   1987

INTERNSHIP EXPERIENCE
Fifth and Sixth Grade Combination Classroom, American Horse Day School, Allen, South Dakota, January - May 1995.
Sixth Grade Language Arts Classroom, Ogallala Middle School Summer Enrichment Program, Ogallala, Nebraska, Summer 1994.
Fourth Grade Open-space Classroom, Field Club Elementary School, Omaha Public Schools, Omaha, Nebraska, Fall 1993.

Teaching highlights included:
Designed curriculum materials that reflect a student-centered approach with many hands-on activities.
Incorporated cross-curricular components into lessons and units. Designed, planned and presented in-depth units on cities, money, measurement, and Native American customs.
Managed three reading groups using both basal materials and literature-based novel units.
Used actual experiences and authentic audiences when teaching reading.
Developed an integrated theme on Plants and Seeds which infused all subject areas with a literature-based approach.
Taught math and bridged the concrete to the abstract through the use of manipulatives and computer activities.

UNIVERSITY UNDERGRADUATE ASSISTANTSHIP
Research Assistant, Young Reader's Book Program, University of Nebraska - Lincoln, Curriculum and Instruction Division, 1993 - 1994. Responsible for reading and reviewing new adolescent books. Prepared bibliographies of the materials for use by teachers and curriculum supervisors in Nebraska.

RELATED WORK EXPERIENCE
House Parent, St. Joseph's Indian School, Chamberlain, South Dakota, 1987 - 1992. Responsibilities included the care of 12 children in the Family Living Unit. Provided both social and life skills training while meeting the physical, spiritual, and emotional needs of the Sioux Indian children. Also assisted with the planning of the summer program. Program included community activities, summer recreation projects and coaching of the swim team.

Data Entry Clerk and Supervisor, Bureau of Indian Affairs, Pierre Area Office, Pierre, South Dakota, 1983 - 1985. Maintained records of 58 tribally-operated schools in a three-state area. Recorded statistics on the number of students enrolled in public schools and reservation areas. Responsible for updating financial support records from the Bureau of Indian Affairs.

References provided upon request.

JAMIE BOND

221 College Street
Any City, State 12345
(101) 555-0009

OBJECTIVE

Teacher: Elementary Education (3-6) or Reading (4-6)

EDUCATION

The University of Iowa, Iowa City, Iowa
  B.S. Degree - May, 1995
    Major: Elementary Education
    Area of Specialization: Reading

COURSE HIGHLIGHTS

Literature for Children	Classroom Management
Language and Society	Multicultural-Bilingual Education
Manual Communication	Microcomputers for the Teacher

STUDENT TEACHING

4th and 5th grades, Shimek Elementary, Iowa City, 9/94-12/94

Responsibilities:
• Attended Madeline Hunter Effectiveness Teacher Training and
  implemented these techniques in daily teaching
• Taught individualized math and three reading groups
• Organized and created learning centers and bulletin boards
• Effectively used cooperative learning strategies
• Implemented and directed computer use in the classroom
• Incorporated Writer's Workshop techniques
• Used higher order thinking strategies
• Team-taught social studies, language arts and science
• Assisted with parent-teacher conferences and open house

Reading Clinic, 4th grade, Lincoln Elementary, Iowa City, 2/95-4/95

Responsibilities:
• Developed, administered and scored an Individualized Reading
  Inventory and Standardized Reading Inventory
• Taught developmental reading to a group of nine fourth graders
• Designed and maintained progress charts
• Conducted a case study
• Communicated with parents on a regular basis
• Attended child study team meetings and staffing for
  learning disabled

RELATED ACTIVITIES

Private tutor, Iowa City, summer, 1994
Hospital volunteer, Pediatrics, University of Iowa Hospitals, 1991-1993
Umpire, Little League, Iowa City, summers, 1991-1993
Member, Old Capitol Area Reading Council

CREDENTIALS

Educational Placement Office, Any City, State 12345
Telephone: (101) 555-0008 FAX: (101) 555-0089

KURT KNIGHT

221 College Street
Any City, State 12345
(101) 555-1111
email:kurt-knight@n.montana.edu

ACADEMIC TRAINING

M.A. Reading, Northern Montana College, Havre, Montana, June 1995
Thesis: Self-Esteem and Reading Ability in First Grade Students
Adviser: Dr. Will B. Prof, Department Chair
B.A. Elementary Education Emphasis: Developmental Reading, May 1993

GRADUATE COURSES OF INTEREST

Building Foundations for Reading:
  Preprimary & Primary
Advanced Reading Clinic Techniques
Developmental Reading Skills

Diagnostic & Prescriptive
  Approaches to Reading K-12
Seminar: Research & Current
  Issues in Reading

CLASSROOM EXPERIENCES

Graduate Internship: Elementary Reading, grades 1-3, Devlin School, Havre, Montana January - May 1995. Worked under the supervision of a master reading clinician. Used the Reading Recovery Model for individual students in the morning and taught in a reading resource room in the afternoons. Five basic instructional activities were utilized: (1) rereading a familiar book; (2) reading a new book; (3) mini-lessons; (4) writing/editing; and (5) introducing a new book. Carefully assessed students' ability, evaluated progress, and communicated on a regular basis with parents and classroom teachers.

Reading Practicum: ESL Classroom, Rocky Boy School, Box Elder, Montana, Spring 1994. Worked in an English as a Second Language classroom teaching reading to two eleven-year-old students, one from Nigeria, the other from Argentina. Used a variety of methods to reach students who were reading at first grade level. Organized basal, word attack, and language experience units.

Student Teacher: Elementary Basic Skills Teacher, Gildford Colony School, Gildford, Montana, Fall 1992. Worked in a rural K-8 school with an enrollment of 16 students. Primary teaching focus was teaching reading and writing. Reading focused on the areas of comprehension, fluency, word identification, and sight vocabulary. Motivated older students to choose own book topics then rehearsed, drafted, shared, revised, edited, and published reports for inclusion in library.

HONORS, ACTIVITIES & AFFILIATIONS

Dean's Achievement Award, College of Education, Northern Montana College
Reed A. Lot Scholarship, Montana Reading Council, 1994
Member, Pi Lambda Theta
Arts Writer, *The Daily Collegian* newspaper, Northern Montana College
Volunteer Campus Tour Guide, Alumni Association, Northern Montana College
Member, International Reading Association
Greater Northern Montana Area Reading Council member
Member, Montana State Reading Association

References provided upon request.

ISABEL ROSSA

221 College Street
Any City, State 12345
(101) 555-0007

TEACHING INTERESTS

Bilingual Early Childhood Special Education Teacher

STUDENT TEACHING INTERNSHIP

<u>Early Childhood Special Education</u>, Educational Service Unit #17,
    Pilot Mountain, North Carolina, November 1993 - May 1994
    Taught eight students in a rural cooperative program. Duties included:
♦ Developed individual plans (IEP), goals and program objectives with regional
  coordinator and parents.
♦ Designed weekly learning activities which corresponded to the IEP goals.
♦ Organized home instruction and incorporated skills across all developmental domains.
♦ Implemented effective behavior management strategies for each student.
♦ Worked closely with the unique circumstances of each family.
♦ Spoke Spanish to communicate and translate information in working with children
  and parents.

<u>Early Childhood Practicum</u>, Peace Preschool of Raleigh, North Carolina August - October 1993
♦ Taught pre-kindergarten students in drama, art activities, and beginning reading.
♦ Assisted with preschool screenings in conjunction with local education professionals.
♦ Planned developmentally appropriate activities for various learning centers.

<u>Preschool Special Education Practicum</u>, Wake County School District, Raleigh, North Carolina,
Mills Elementary, March - May 1993
♦ Worked with four students ages two to four years old in all skill areas.
♦ Assessed students' strengths and designed and implemented a program for each child.

ACADEMIC PREPARATION

Meredith College Raleigh, North Carolina	May 1994	B.A.	Special Education Early Childhood
Nash Community College Rocky Mount, North Carolina	1985	A.A.	Education and Spanish
American School of Torreón Torreón, Mexico	1981	Diploma	

RELATED EMPLOYMENT

<u>Day Care Director and Owner</u>, Rocky Mount, North Carolina, 1985 - 1991
Operated and directed a state licensed day care for infants through kindergarten children.
Supervised staff of six teachers and four paraprofessionals.

<u>Preschool Teacher</u>, Centro para Niños, Torreón, Mexico, 1981 - 1983
Taught in a state operated child care center in Torreón, Mexico. Worked closely with parents
and community agencies to provide appropriate health care and follow-up for children. Spanish
was the primary language of instruction and parental communication.

CREDENTIALS
Career Advising and Placement Center, Any City, State 12345
Telephone: (101) 555-0008 Fax: (101) 555-0089

PATRICK FINNEGAN
221 College Street
Any City, State 12345
(101) 555-0009

EDUCATION

B.S. - Special Education - Elementary Hearing Impaired
Cleveland State University, Cleveland, Ohio, 1990-1994

Deaf Interpreter Training, Summer 1994-present
Gallaudet University, Washington, D.C.

RELATED EXPERIENCE

Student Teaching
Alexander Graham Bell School, Cleveland, Ohio, January - May, 1994
Planned and presented lessons in reading, language arts, and mathematics, emphasizing total communication through an aural-oral approach. Students ranged in age from seven to ten years, in ungraded classrooms. Participated with cooperating teacher and other team members in home visits and parent conferences. Observed and assisted with new student entrance and placement tests.

Practicum Experience
Alexander Graham Bell School, September - December, 1993
Assisted with skills development in reading and mathematics. Provided individualized instruction in manual communication and fingerspelling. Assisted with parent-infant program for children up to three years of age.

RELATED ACTIVITIES

Camp Counselor, Camp for the Deaf, Nanjemoy, Maryland, Summers, 1991-1993
Responsible for day-to-day supervision of six campers including deaf boys and their hearing brothers. Instructor for archery and volleyball, assisted with other activities including biking and basketball.

Volunteer Interpreter, Fairview General Hospital, Cleveland, Ohio, 1991-1994
Interpreter for hearing-impaired patients or relatives to facilitate communication with medical staff. Interpreting assignments arranged through the Department of Speech Pathology and Audiology, Cleveland State University.

MEMBERSHIPS

Alexander Graham Bell Association for the Deaf
Convention of American Instructors of the Deaf
Student Member, Ohio Education Association
Phi Kappa Alpha Fraternity

CREDENTIALS

Career Services Center
Any City, State, 12345
(101) 555-0008

DANA RINGO
221 College Street
Any City, State 12345
(101) 555-0009 (home)
(101) 545-0005 (school)

ACADEMIC BACKGROUND:

Wagner College, Staten Island, New York
   Bachelor of Science Degree, Special Education, 1991-1995
Universidad Granada, Granada, Spain
   Spanish Language and Literature, 1992

   Licensure: **K-6 Special Education, Mild and Moderate Disabilities**
   State of New York

TEACHING INTERNSHIP EXPERIENCE:

Wright School, Brooklyn Borough District 18, Brooklyn, New York, Fall 1995
   Mental Disabilities, Primary Unit
   Taught twelve students with various mental disabilities ranging in ages from
   six to eight years of age. Worked with students in all skill areas; main
   emphasis was on concept development, language, and motor and self-help
   skills. Organized students in instructional groups and worked effectively with
   the child study team. Attended weekly staff meetings, participated in parent
   conferences, and initiated special parent newsletter.

PRACTICA EXPERIENCE:

University Hospital School, Brooklyn, New York, 1994
   Individual work with a twelve-year-old autistic child
Rosa Parks Elementary, Harlem Summer School Program, Harlem, New York 1993
   Taught fifth grade students with limited English skills
Fifth Street Developmental Center, Brooklyn, New York, 1992
   Assisted severely handicapped students with communication skills

COLLEGE DISTINCTIONS & MEMBERSHIPS:

President-elect, International Student Club
A.Z. Zolinsky Memorial Award Scholarship
Member, College of Education Student Advisory Committee
Member, American Federation of Teachers
Member, Council for Exceptional Children

VOLUNTEER AND RELATED WORK EXPERIENCE:

Behavior Disorders Teacher Associate, Brooklyn Opportunity School, Summer, 1994
Spanish Interpreter, St. Pius Hospital Emergency Room, (weekends) 1993 - present
Volunteer, Special Olympics Track Festival, Staten Island, 1991-1993

REFERENCES AVAILABLE UPON REQUEST AT
Placement and Teacher Certification
Any City, State 12345
(101) 555-0008 FAX: (101) 555-1118

CLAIRE GRANT

221 College Street
Any City, State 12345
(101) 555-0009

OBJECTIVE

K-12 Substitute Teacher

EDUCATION

University of Texas at Dallas, Richardson, Texas
    B.A. Degree - May 1994
        Double Major: English and Elementary Education
        Area of Specialization: Middle School

COURSE
HIGHLIGHTS

Classroom Computer Usage	Teacher-Parent Communication
Exceptional Persons	Methods in Bilingual Education
Classroom Management	Special Education Issues

EXPERIENCE

Student Teacher, Wilson Middle School, Dallas, Texas, Fall 1993
    Responsibilities included teaching various units in sixth,
    seventh, and eighth grade. Participated in a five member
    multidisciplinary team using the mastery teaching approach.
    Worked with a diverse student population representing over
    twenty different countries.

Writing Tutor, Wilken Elementary, Richardson, Texas, Summer 1993
    Responsibilities included working with attention deficit
    disordered students in the writing lab. Developed and maintained
    progress reports and communicated with parents regularly.

Practicum Student, South High School, Dallas, Texas, Spring 1992
    Observed and assisted in ninth grade general English.

Composition Evaluator, Macmillan/McGraw-Hill, Houston, Texas
    Summers 1993 - present
    Evaluate eighth grade compositions for the Indiana State Testing
    of Education Progress. (Seasonal employment)

RELATED
ACTIVITIES

Youth Support Services, Pen Pal Partner, Summers 1991-1993
Asian Community Center Volunteer, 1989 - present
Member, National Council of Teachers of English
Member, National Association for Young Children

CREDENTIALS

Career Planning & Placement Center
Any City, State 12345 Telephone: (101) 555-0008

SCOTT HARRIS

221 College Street
Any City, State 12345
(101) 555-0009

OBJECTIVE	**Teacher:** Secondary Agriculture Education
EDUCATION	Purdue University, West Lafayette, Indiana B.S. Degree - May 1995 Major: Agriculture Education Teaching Certificate, Grades 7 - 12, May 1995 Indiana Vocational Technical College-Lafayette Associate's Degree - Agricultural Technologies, 1990
STUDENT TEACHING	**Agriculture Education**, South Putnam H.S., Greencastle, Indiana Responsibilities: • Developed and taught units on soil analysis and farm management • Team taught two-week ecology unit with biology teacher • Assisted sponsor of Future Farmers of America with planning and supervision of club activities and fundraisers • Graded FFA Proficiency Applications
RELATED EMPLOYMENT	**Field research assistant**, King Hybrid Seed Company, Vincennes, Indiana summers, 1994, 1995 **Family farm worker**, 12 years experience
ACTIVITIES & AWARDS	• Judged FFA Leadership Contests • Future Farmers of America Scholarship • Dean's list, 5 semesters
MEMBERSHIPS	• Student Member, Indiana Vocational Agriculture Teachers Association Secretary, Purdue Chapter, 1994-1995 Program Planning Committee Member, 1995 • National Vocational Agriculture Teachers Association • 4-H Member, 10 years; Officer, 4 years
CREDENTIALS ON FILE	Office of Educational Placement Any City, State 12345 (101) 555-0008

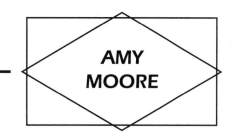

AMY MOORE

221 College Street, Any City, State 12345 (101) 555-0009

TEACHING OBJECTIVE
 • Art teacher, grades K-12

EDUCATION
 Bachelor of Fine Arts Major: *Art* Studio Emphasis: *Printmaking*
 Duquesne University, Pittsburgh, Pennsylvania May 1995
  • Dean's List
  • Art Education Scholarship

TEACHING EXPERIENCE
 High School Art: Student teacher, Pittsburgh Public Schools, Fall semester, 1995
  Prepared educational objectives and lesson plans for painting, drawing,
  sculpture, and jewelry courses at Hoover High School. Assisted with
  teaching responsibilities in photography. Organized student exhibits at the
  high school and the city art museum. Submitted student work for
  consideration in the Philadelphia Young Artist's Review. Attended faculty
  meetings, participated in school improvement team meetings and
  volunteered at school functions.

 Elementary Art: Student teacher, E.J. Parks Elementary, Pittsburgh, Spring 1994
  Taught art at four different grade levels. Created units in bookmaking, pop-
  ups, multimedia, pottery, fabric design and multicultural units on Egypt and
  Mexico. Exhibited student artwork in library, display cases, hallways and
  classrooms. Evaluated students' work and offered before-school art sessions
  for additional help. Involved in interdisciplinary team teaching.

RELATED ART EXPERIENCE
 Saturday Morning Art Workshop, Duquesne University, Fall 1994
 Volunteer Art Tutor, Eastside Youth Project, Pittsburgh, 1991-1993
 High School Painting Workshop, Pittsburgh Alternative Center, 1993
 Artist in Residence, North High School, Philadelphia Public Schools, 1992

PROFESSIONAL ORGANIZATIONS
 National Art Education Association
 Handweavers Guild of America
 Women's Caucus for Art
 National Education Association

CREDENTIALS ON FILE
Career Planning & Placement Center
Any City, State 12345 Telephone: (101) 555-0008

KELLY McCABE
221 College Street
Any City, State 12345
(101) 555-0009

Teaching Interests

HIGH SCHOOL BUSINESS EDUCATION

Keyboarding	Word Processing	Business Office Machines
Desktop Publishing	Spreadsheets	Consumer Mathematics

Education

Walla Walla College, College Place, Washington, Bachelor's Degree, 1995
Major: Business Education   Minor: Mathematics

Student Teaching Experience

Business Education, Waitsburg High School, Waitsburg, Washington, Spring 1995

Taught courses in personal computer applications and keyboarding.
Observed and assisted with basic and advanced word processing courses.
Worked with students of diverse backgrounds and varying degrees of experience
   with computer applications, individually and in small and large groups.
Arranged (with supervision from cooperating teacher) for a class visit to a
   regional office technology fair in Spokane, Washington.
Assisted with layout of student newspaper, using PCL and PostScript.
Participated in mid-semester parent conferences.
Co-sponsored student-initiated recycling project.

Practicum Experience

Computer Applications, Walla Walla High School, Spring 1994

Consumer Mathematics, Garrison Junior High School, Spring 1994

Office Technology, Walla Walla High School, Fall 1993

Related Employment

Publications Clerk (work-study position), Public Relations, Walla Walla College, 1993-1994

Assist with word processing for publications including news releases, and page layout for
recruitment brochures and admissions information using PageMaker.

Current Activities & Affiliations

Secretary, Walla Walla College chapter, Student Business Educators' Association
Student representative, faculty search committee
Student Member, Washington State Education Association
Volunteer, Walla Walla County Wildlife Society

Credentials

Office of Career Planning
Any City, State 12345 (101) 555-0008

KIRK VAN METER

221 College Street   Any City, State 12345   (101) 555-0009

EDUCATION

Secondary Certification - Business and Cooperative Education - August, 1994
Michigan State University, East Lansing, Michigan

B.S. - Business Administration - December, 1988
Wayne State University, Detroit, Michigan

INTERNSHIP EXPERIENCE

Battle Creek High School, Battle Creek, Michigan, January - May, 1994

Sixteen-week internship provided opportunity to work with faculty coordinators to develop student goals and objectives for work experiences; assist students in preparing for the work experience including resume writing, work ethics, introduction to the business environment, and interviewing skills workshops. Assisted in developing and conducting student, worksite, and program evaluations. Visited businesses and industries to initiate and promote student placements and to develop future training sites.

RELATED EXPERIENCE

Assistant Director of Human Resources, Michigan Educators Insurance Agency, Auburn Hills, Michigan - 1990-1993

Training Supervisor, Goodwill Industries, Lansing, Michigan - 1988-1990

ACTIVITIES

Volunteer, Lansing Big Brothers Association
Baseball Coach, Lansing Babe Ruth League
Membership Chairperson, Lansing Community Theater
Member, United Action for Youth
Volunteer, March of Dimes Marathon

REFERENCES

Credentials available from Career Development & Placement Services
Any City, State 12345   (101) 555-0008

CHELSEA ROBBINS

221 College Street
Any City, State 12345
(101) 555-0009

OBJECTIVE
Teacher - English as a Second Language

ACADEMIC TRAINING

Advanced Studies - Linguistics, University of the South, Sewanee, Tennessee, 1994 - 1995

B.A. - German, Japanese minor, Miami University, Miami, Ohio, 1989-1993

LANGUAGE BACKGROUND

German:	36 semester hours at Miami University Participated in a six-month advanced language program in Austria Four years of German in high school AFS Student to Karlstadt, Germany, junior year of high school
Japanese:	24 semester hours in Japanese language and culture Worked extensively with a Japanese tutor to enhance speaking skills Traveled to Japan, Summer, 1992
Travel & Study Abroad:	Extensive travel in Europe and Japan on four different occasions • Studied at the Regents Summer Program in Austria, 1991 • Intensive language study in St. Radegund • Advanced language study, University of Vienna Hochschulekurs
Other Language Experience:	Resided for three years in the Miami Foreign Language Residence Hall • Involved in various intercultural exchanges with foreign students from Japan, Germany, China, Nepal, Brazil, France, Syria, and other countries • Participated in campus presentations and public intercultural activities • Shared experiences and language study with other students who have lived abroad or traveled extensively

TEACHING EXPERIENCE

Student Teaching:	Stowe Senior High School, Sewanee, Tennessee, and Wells Elementary School, Winchester, Tennessee, Spring, 1995 English language assessment and instruction for children with limited or no English language skills from fifteen different countries
Practicum:	Burford Intermediate School, Chattanooga, Tennessee, Fall 1994 Assisted with instruction of two classes of Introductory German, grade 6, and two classes of 7th grade German. Worked with students individually and in small groups.
Language Lab Attendant:	University of the South, 1994 - present Assisted users with language lab technology, answered questions, provided students with resources to complete assignments, and monitored lab equipment.

Credentials available from Career Planning and Placement Center
Any City, State 12345 Telephone: (101) 555-0008

EDWARD HOFFMAN

221 College Street
Any City, State 12345
(101) 555-0009

OBJECTIVE	**High School English Instructor** **Speech and Drama Director**
DEGREES	**Master of Arts in Teaching**, English Education Indiana University, Bloomington, Indiana, 12/95 **Bachelor of Arts**, double major in English and Speech Coe College, Cedar Rapids, Iowa, 5/93
STUDENT TEACHING	**High School English**, Jefferson High School Bloomington, Indiana 8/95-10/95 **Middle School and High School English**, The American School of Japan Tokyo, Japan, 10/95-12/95 *Responsibilities of the above positions included preparation of educational objectives and lesson plans for three grade levels. Instructed a middle school special reading course, 10th grade American Literature and Language class and an elective speech course for juniors and seniors. Supervised students in the computer writing lab and initiated special study review sessions.*
SPEECH & DRAMA	**Volunteer Speech Assistant**, Solon High School, Solon, Iowa, 9/92-5/93 *Assisted with play productions and coached members of the speech team involved in interpretation events. Traveled to meets and supervised students.* **8th grade Speech**, Practicum teaching experience, Southeast Junior High School, Bloomington, Indiana 10/94 - 12/94 *Worked with three sections of students in an elective speech class. Led small group discussions and worked with students on an individual basis.*
RELATED ACTIVITIES	**Actor**, Indiana Players Repertory Company **Actor**, Bloomington Community Theatre **Stage hand**, Hoosier Auditorium
PART-TIME EXPERIENCE	Member, Hoosier Usher Corps, Indiana Center for the Arts, 1992-1995 Cashier, Indiana University Book & Supply, 1994 Library Clerk, Coe College Library, 1990-1993 *(Financed schooling through part-time employment and loans)*
PROFESSIONAL AFFILIATIONS	Indiana Communication Association Speech Communication Association National Council of Teachers of English
CREDENTIALS	Educational Placement Office Any City, State 12345-1338 (101) 555-0008

JENNIFER KIDWELL

221 College Street
Any City, State 12345
(101) 555-0009

TEACHING STRENGTHS

- World History
- European History

- Government
- Geography

Will direct or assist in student government,
model UN, debate, and class sponsorship

ACADEMIC BACKGROUND

History - B.A. *(with distinction)* - 1994
   University of Southern Colorado, Pueblo, Colorado

STUDENT TEACHING EXPERIENCE

Poudre School District, Fort Collins, Colorado, Fall, 1994
Secondary Social Studies.
Prepared educational objectives and lesson plans for three levels. Worked with individuals, small groups, and large groups using a variety of teaching strategies. Conducted after-school study and tutoring sessions. Student teaching consisted of a full-day, full-semester experience. Worked extensively with the following three classes:

- *Africa and Latin America*: used simulations, media, guest speakers, and small group activities to familiarize students with issues and problems confronting lesser-developed countries (LDCs). Topics included debt, development, environment, and international relations. Concentrated on verbal and critical thinking skills.

- *World History*: taught medieval history to remedial students. Developed a major unit on the concept of nation-building. Concentrated on improving students' study skills.

- *European History*: taught ancient and medieval European history to tenth and eleventh graders. Prepared and taught a unit on castles and serfdom. Concentrated on students' research and writing skills.

RELATED EXPERIENCE

Middle School Social Studies, practicum, Franklin Middle School, Pueblo, Spring 1992
Tutor, Community Center Adult Learning Program, Pueblo, 1991-present
Crisis Center Volunteer, Crisis Center, Pueblo, 1992-present
Big Brother/Big Sister Partner, Pueblo, 1991, 1993

CREDENTIALS

Education Placement Office, Any City, State 12345
Telephone: (101) 555-0008 FAX: (101) 555-0089

SARA SWANN
221 College Street
Anytown, State 12345
(101) 555-0009

TEACHING COMPETENCIES

Home Economics
Life Skills
Home Computer Usage
Interior Design

Health
Substance Abuse
Disease Prevention
Consumer Health

EXTRACURRICULAR INTERESTS

Medical Sciences Club
International Student Advisor

Class Sponsor
Yearbook Advisor

ACADEMIC TRAINING

University of Georgia
Athens, Georgia

Teacher Certification
December, 1995

Home Economics

Chicago State University
Chicago, Illinois

Bachelor of Science
May, 1993

Major: Science
Major: Health

STUDENT TEACHING

Home Economics, Northwest High School, Atlanta Public Schools, fall 1995
Responsibilities included teaching units in the following classes:
- Independent Living
- Family Planning
- Interior Design
- Issues in Health

PRACTICA EXPERIENCE

Middle School Health, Sauk Middle School, Atlanta, spring 1994
- Assisted with teaching responsibilities in health, grades 6 - 8
- Led small group activities and organized group follow-up sessions
- Developed a unit on personal health care and sex education
- Volunteered to supervise after-school study lab

Elementary Health, Grant Elementary, Chicago Public Schools, spring 1993
- Created a multi-disciplinary unit on drugs and their consequences
- Invited a doctor to talk to students about addiction and lifelong effects

OTHER WORK EXPERIENCE

Tutor - Regional Services for Youth Organization, Athens, 1995
Counselor for terminally ill children - Camp Sunbreak, Miami, summers 1990-1991
Day care provider - Emergency Child Care Services of Chicago, 1989-1993

CREDENTIALS

Career Planning and Placement, Any City, State 12345 (101) 555-0008

JOHN DUBACH
221 College Street
Any City, State 12345
(101) 555-0009

TEACHING EXPERIENCE

Vocational Environmental Horticulture Teacher, 1992-Present
Olympia Public Schools, Olympia, Washington
o Teach Introduction to Horticulture, Environmental Horticulture, and Advanced Horticulture in a sequential, competency-based program
o Work with students from diverse backgrounds, including special needs, special education, and ESL students
o Develop and supervise student occupational experiences
o Prepare and monitor program budget
o Maintain inventory of supplies
o Sponsor and maintain active chapter of Future Farmers of America

RELATED EXPERIENCE

Horticultural Worker, 1988-1991; Summers 1983-1988
Stone Mountain Nursery, Olympia Washington
o Assisted with all areas of greenhouse and nursery operations
o Prepared cost and labor estimates for landscape gardening projects
o Experience with marketing and retail sales

EDUCATION

Washington State University, Pullman, Washington
    Teacher Certification: Vocational Agriculture, 1992
    Bachelor of Science Degree: Horticulture, 1988

AWARDS

Nominee, Thurston County Vocational Educator Award, 1994
Named Outstanding Horticulture Student, 1987
Dean's List, Washington State University - 3 years
Future Farmers of America Scholarship, 1985

REFERENCES

Complete placement file available from Career Services
Any City, State 12345
(101) 555-0008 FAX: (101) 555-0089

KEVIN KLADDE
221 College Street
Any City, State 12345
(101) 555-0009

EDUCATION	B.S. Degree - Industrial Arts Education - May 1995 University of Wisconsin - Platteville, Platteville, Wisconsin

TEACHING INTERESTS

Technical Drawing	Basic Wood Technology
Architectural Drawing	Advanced Wood Technology
Construction Technology	Home Maintenance

COACHING INTERESTS

Golf	Assist with:
Track & Field	Baseball, Basketball, Soccer

STUDENT TEACHING

Industrial Technology, Fall 1994, River Valley High School, Spring Green, Wisconsin
• Planned and presented units on using hand tools and basic carpentry for a one-semester Home and Auto Repair course
• Taught drafting exercises including dimensioning, sectional views, pictorials, and architectural floor plan design
• Assisted with computer aided drafting and design
• Worked with individualized and group projects in technical drawing
• On-site supervisor for electrical wiring at student home construction project
• Helped organize annual student project exhibit for all woodworking and metalcraft classes

RELATED ACTIVITIES

Assistant Track Coach, River Valley High School, Spring 1995
Softball Coach, Platteville Parks Program, 1992-1994
Golf Team, University of Wisconsin-Platteville, 1991-1994

RELATED EMPLOYMENT

Construction Worker, Emerson Developers, Monroe, Wisconsin
Summers 1991-1994

MEMBERSHIPS

Student Member, Wisconsin Industrial Arts Teachers Association
Student Member, Wisconsin Education Association
Corresponding Secretary, local chapter, Wisconsin Antique Auto Club
Citizen Action Network
Sierra Club

CREDENTIALS ON FILE

Teacher Placement Office
Any City, State 12345 (101) 555-0008

JILL
—— HAWKES ——

221 College Street, Any City, State 12345, (101) 555-0009 (home)
(101) 555-1111 (business)

OBJECTIVE:
Journalism teacher and student newspaper advisor.

CURRENT PROFESSIONAL EXPERIENCE:
Staff Writer, Daily Times, Montgomery, Alabama, present.
Responsible for covering education and city hall news. Supervise students participating
in the High School Reporting Internships Program sponsored by the *Daily Times.*

EDUCATIONAL FIELD EXPERIENCES:
Journalism Student Teacher, Montgomery Public Schools, fall semester 1995
Journalism Intern, Huntsville City Schools, spring semester 1994

Responsibilities included teaching classes in Foundations of Journalistic Writing
and Advertising and Mass Media Lab and Newsmagazine Lab. Worked extensively
with students in the newspaper lab teaching journalistic writing, design, desktop
publishing, editing and paste-up. Assisted students in selling ads for the newspaper.

GRADUATE COURSE CONCENTRATIONS:
Media and Consumers
Editing Workshop
Gender and Mass Communication
Journalistic Writing and Reporting
Legal and Ethical Issues in Communication
Publication Design Workshop

ACADEMIC TRAINING:
Master of Arts Degree
School of Journalism and Mass Communication
Alabama State University, Montgomery, 1995

Bachelor of Science Degree
Journalism Major, Global Studies Minor
Auburn University, Auburn, Alabama, 1991

PROFESSIONAL ASSOCIATIONS:
National Association of Hispanic Journalists
American Society of Journalists and Authors
Association for Education in Journalism and Mass Communication

PRESENTATIONS:
"Teaching Students their Rights as Young Editors," pre-conference workshop presentation,
Association for Education in Journalism and Mass Communication, New Orleans,
Louisiana, August 1994
"Newspaper Labs in High Schools: Partnerships with Local Newspapers," address at State
Conference for High School Journalism Teachers, Atlanta, Georgia, May 1994.
Panel member, "Ethics in Reporting: Whose Ethics?" Investigative Reporters and Editors
Conference, West Palm Beach, Florida, October 1993.

REFERENCES:
Furnished Upon Request

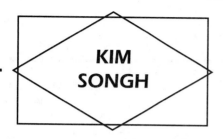

KIM SONGH

221 College Street, Any City, State 12345 (101) 555-0009

TEACHING COMPETENCIES
- Algebra and Geometry
- Trigonometry and Finite Mathematics
- Advanced Algebra and Calculus
- General Mathematics
- Computer Science
- Statistics and Measurement

EDUCATION
Teacher Certification Program, Mathematics, 8/95
Marquette University, Milwaukee, Wisconsin

Bachelor of Science Degree, Major: Mathematics
Virginia State University, Chesterfield, Virginia, 1990-1993
- Dean's List
- Presidential Citation

CLASSROOM TEACHING EXPERIENCE
Internship: High School Math. Kansas City Public Schools, Kansas City, Kansas
1/95 - 5/95
Work as a teacher intern in an inner-city magnet school teaching algebra, geometry and calculus. Use a variety of teaching and motivational strategies to encourage students to reach their potential. Volunteer supervisor of Math Club, Computer Programming Club and College Bowl.

Practicum: Elementary Math. Longfellow Elementary, Milwaukee, Wisconsin
10/94 - 12/94
Taught in a 5/6th combination classroom with students of varied abilities. Designed special activities to demonstrate math concepts and used the computer to reinforce material. Involved in various inservice meetings and school events and participated in weekend parent-teacher conferences.

RELATED EXPERIENCE
Computer Tutor, Milwaukee and Kansas City, 1993-present.
Resident Assistant, Virginia State University, 1991-1993.
Camp Counselor, Camp Pine Oaks, for at-risk 10-12 year olds, Nine Springs, Colorado, summers, 1989-1991.

PROFESSIONAL ORGANIZATIONS
Missouri Council of Teachers of Mathematics
National Council of Teachers of Mathematics
National Education Association

CREDENTIALS ON FILE
Career Services Center
Any City, State 12345 (101) 555-0008

AHMED KHAN
221 College Street
Any City, State 12345
(101) 555-0009

EDUCATION

B.A. - Education - Language Arts and Social Studies Emphasis - 1994
Rhode Island College, Providence, Rhode Island

STUDENT TEACHING

Esek Hopkins Middle School, Providence, Rhode Island, February - June, 1994
• Team teaching in integrated Language Arts/Social Studies program, grades 5-6
• Developed writing skills using a "writers workshop" mode of instruction
• Prepared units on history and biographies of the colonial period
• Created bulletin boards and interest centers to emphasize contributions of women
     to colonial social and cultural history
• Practiced effective classroom management techniques to promote student achievement
• Devised projects for individual investigation and small group collaboration suitable
     for students with a wide range of interests and achievement levels
• Assisted with supervision of pupils in out-of-classroom activities
• Participated in grade level curriculum and team meetings
• Attended and participated in parent conferences to discuss student progress and to
     interpret school programs and expectations

PRACTICUM EXPERIENCE

Oliver Hazard Perry Middle School, Providence, Rhode Island, September-October, 1993
• Observed and participated in language arts instruction; worked with individual students on
     vocabulary building and improving reading skills; volunteered to assist with layout
     of magazine featuring student prose, poetry, and art work.
Urban Collaborative Accelerated Program, Providence, Rhode Island, April-May, 1993
• Observed team of three teachers employing an integrated approach to language arts and social
     studies instruction with students of exceptional abilities and a wide range of interests;
     observed team planning and evaluation sessions.

RELATED ACTIVITIES

Playground and Cafeteria Monitor, Mary E. Fogarty School, Providence, Rhode Island, 1991-1993
     Supervised lunchroom and playground behavior of elementary students (K-6) to
     ensure and promote safety and consideration for other students.

MEMBERSHIPS

Rhode Island Student Education Association
Institute for Democracy in Education Association
Rhode Island College Society for Creative Anachronism
Volunteer, Student Cooperative Bookstore

CREDENTIALS

Career Development Center
Any City, State, 12345
(101) 555-0008

JOSHUA HATCHER
221 College Street
Any City, State 12345
(101) 555-1111

DEGREES

M.A. English Education, The Pennsylvania State University, University Park, June 1995
   Thesis: Assessment of Skills Development in Portfolios of Student Writing
   Adviser: Dr. Willa Pruvitt, Department Chair
B.A. English Education Emphases: Language Arts and Middle School Education, May 1992

CLASSROOM EXPERIENCE

Middle School Language Arts Student Teaching Internship, Hannah Middle School, York, Pennsylvania, October 1994 - May 1995. Taught in heterogeneous multi-ethnic classrooms consisting of students at all learning levels. Participated in the middle school team approach to teaching and prepared interdisciplinary units and lessons. Incorporated cooperative learning activities into the curriculum and provided peer tutoring services for students needing additional help. Initiated the development of writing portfolios and regular conferences with individual students.

English 9 Practicum Experience, Elk Lake Junior Senior High School, Dimock, Pennsylvania, Spring 1992. Worked with required language arts courses teaching thematic units centered around survival, handicaps, and fantasy incorporating poetry, prose and drama. Established daily journal writing in class and also integrated whole language reading and writing activities within established curriculum.

Seventh Grade Language Arts Observation Class, Indian Valley Middle School, Reedsville, Pennsylvania, Fall 1991. Assisted mentor teacher with implementation of a writing workshop. Taught mini-lessons on elements of process writing and incorporated grammar and spelling skills into a whole language approach to teaching writing.

VOLUNTEER TEACHING EXPERIENCE

Volunteer English as a Second Language Instructor, Czech Republic (Sponsored by Education For Democracy/U.S.A., Inc.) September 1992 - August 1993. Taught English conversation and grammar to elementary students in a local grammar school. Responsibilities included developing curriculum and teaching materials.

RELATED EXPERIENCE

National Outdoor Leadership School, Lander, Wyoming
   Summer Program, 1994
   Participated in a five-week wilderness and mountaineering expedition in the Rockies of Wyoming. Activities included skills training, leadership development, backpacking, rock climbing, snow and glacier travel, and fly-fishing.
Herencia Espanola, Madrid University, Madrid, Spain
   Summer Study Program, 1991
   Participated in 60 hours of Spanish language and culture classes and a week of travel through Spain. Lived in dormitories with students from over 30 countries.
River City Orchestra Camp, East St. Louis, Illinois
   Camp Counselor, Summers 1989 and 1990
   Responsible for the supervision of twelve junior high orchestra campers. Organized swimming, volleyball, ping-pong, and other recreational activities for campers after recitals, concerts, and rehearsals.

CREDENTIALS

Career Placement and Services Center, Any City, State 12345   Telephone (101)555-0008

MELISSA REID

221 College Street
Any City, State 12345
(101) 555-0009

OBJECTIVE

Middle School Reading Teacher

EDUCATION

Old Dominion University, Norfolk, Virginia
  B.A. Degree - June, 1995
    Major: Reading

Université de Leon, Leon, France
  Year Abroad Program, 1994
    Emphases: Literature and Art

COURSE HIGHLIGHTS

Methods: High School Reading   Diagnostic Techniques
Literature for Children   Research and Current Issues in Reading
Reading Clinic   Building Foundations for Reading

EXPERIENCE

Teaching Internship:
<u>Middle School Developmental Reading</u>, Norfolk Public Schools, 1/94 - 6/95
  Major areas of teaching and related activities included:
    •Word identification
    •Sight vocabulary
    •Comprehension
    •Fluency
    •Integrating of reading and writing
    •Self-selected reading

Practica:
<u>High School Reading</u>, (9th grade), Metro Alternative Center, Norfolk
    Fall semester, 1994
<u>Intermediate Grade Reading</u>, Edison Elementary School, Norfolk
    Spring semester, 1994
<u>Advanced Reading for Gifted Students</u>, (3rd grade), St. Lukes Academy, Summer, 1993

Travel & Language Ability:
Lived with a French family, 1994
Traveled extensively in Europe
Fluent in French

RELATED ACTIVITIES

Pen Pal Partner, Norfolk Neighborhood Projects, 1992-1995
Reader for the Blind, Old Dominion Special Services, 1994
Volunteer reader for local senior citizens' center, 1993
International Reading Association, Member

CREDENTIALS

Educational Career Services, Any City, State 12345   (101) 555-0008

PETER WELCHER
221 College Street
Any City, State 12345
(101) 555-0009

OBJECTIVE:	**Middle School Tech Lab Instructor**

DEGREES:

University of Oklahoma, Norman, Oklahoma
    Bachelor of Science Degree - May 1995
      Major: Computer Science

Oklahoma Junior College of Business and Technology, Tulsa, Oklahoma
    Associate Degree - June 1990
      Area: Electronics

FIELD EXPERIENCES:
(1995)

Student Teacher - Technology Lab, Irving Middle School, Norman, Oklahoma
Practicum Teacher - Computer Lab, Little Axe High School, Norman, Oklahoma
Methods Class - Electronics Class, Senior High School, Norman, Oklahoma

<u>Student teaching responsibilities included:</u>
Teaching computer assisted instruction in a number of tech modules
in a newly established technology lab. Modules included hands-on
applications in electronics, transportation manufacturing, hydraulics,
drafting, robotics, engineering, and audio-visual productions.
Student-centered modules were designed to provide realistic experiences
and career related information.

WORK EXPERIENCE:

Electronics Specialist, Oklahoma Light and Power Company, Tulsa, Oklahoma
    1987 - 1991

Electronics Apprentice, Tulsa Lighting Company, Tulsa, Oklahoma
    1985 - 1987

Semi-truck Driver, Monfort Trucking, Denver, Colorado
    1978 - 1980

MILITARY:

U. S. Navy, Electronic Specialist, 1980 - 1984
    Served on the battleships U.S.S. Missouri and Iowa
    Tours included the Pacific Rim and the Persian Gulf area

INTERESTS:

Model airplanes (President of local Model Airplane Association)
Antique Auto Repair
Private Flight Instructor

CREDENTIALS ON FILE:

Teacher Career Center
Any City, State 12345 (101) 555-0008

ERIKA NIELSEN

221 College Street, Any City, State 12345   (101) 555-0009

Teaching Competencies

VOCAL
Concert and Swing Choirs
Choir (7th-12th)
Vocal Instruction
Ensembles

Special Interests

Contest Entries
All-State Participation

State and Regional Contests
Music Fund-raising Club

Academic Training

University of Alaska-Fairbanks
Fairbanks, Alaska

Teacher Certification: Music
December, 1995

Arizona State University
Tempe, Arizona

B.M. 1993
Major: Music   Minor: Math

Student Teaching

H.S. Music, Yukon Flats High School, Beaver, Alaska, fall 1995
- Taught instrumental and vocal music appreciation classes
- Prepared lesson plans and objectives using the teacher effectiveness model
- Encouraged students to participate in music opportunities
- Provided tutorial services for students wishing advanced training
- Incorporated cultural songs and special native Alaskan activities into classes
- Evaluated student progress by offering private lessons and small group practice sessions
- Performed local concerts and participated in regional contests
- Attended inservice sessions, faculty meetings and school functions

Practicum Experience

Middle School Vocal Music, Yukon Middle School, Arctic Flats, Alaska, spring 1994
- Assisted with teaching responsibilities in general music classes and choir
- Worked with small group music ensembles
- Reviewed music curriculum and related teaching materials

Activities & Awards

University Concert Choir, Arizona State, 4 years
Leading singing roles in two operas, Arizona State, 2 years
Performed in numerous musicals and concerts, 4 years
Arizona State Music Scholarship, 3 years, and Dean's List, 7 semesters

Other Work Experience

All-State Music Instructor - Arizona State University Summer Camp, 1994
Private music lessons - Tempe and Fairbanks area, summers 1989-present
Keyboard Music Sales Associate - Fairbanks, part-time present

Credentials at Teacher Placement Center, Any City, State 12345
Telephone: (101) 555-0008; FAX: (101) 555-1118

NICHOLAS TRESNAK

221 College Street
Any City, State 12345
(101) 555-0009

OBJECTIVE:

Physical Education Instructor, grades K-12
Adaptive Physical Education Instructor, Middle School
Extracurricular interests in coaching men's or women's tennis

EDUCATION:

Iowa State University, Ames, Iowa
    Bachelor of Science Degree - May 1995
    Major: Exercise Science with emphasis in Physical Education
    Minor: Special Education

LICENSURE:

Iowa Professional Teaching License, Physical Education, grades K-12
Adaptive Physical Education Endorsement, grades K-8
State of Iowa Coaching Authorization

TEACHING INTERNSHIPS:

Elementary Physical Education, Edwards Elementary School, Ames, Iowa, 8/94 - 10/94
High School Physical Education, Ames High School, Ames, Iowa, 10/94 - 12/94
Adaptive Physical Education, Nevada Middle School, Nevada, Iowa, 1/95 - 3/95
Responsibilities:
- Taught students at all levels from kindergarten to high school seniors.
- Used various teaching techniques to allow for differing learning styles.
- Worked with adaptive physical education students and developed appropriate skill-level activities.
- Established an active learning environment through positive feedback.
- Assisted with the organization of the Heart Association's Jump Rope for Heart.
- Observed special education classes and met with teachers to better serve adaptive physical education students.
- Participated in coordination of the Fine Arts Festival at Edwards Elementary.

PRACTICA:

Special Education, Ames Middle School, Ames, Iowa, Fall 1993
Adaptive Physical Education, Parkview Middle School, Ankeny, Iowa, Fall 1993
Health Education, Ankeny High School, Ankeny, Iowa, Spring 1992
Physical Education, Ames High School, Ames, Iowa, Fall 1992

COACHING:

Tennis, Club Coach for University Athletic Club, Ames, Iowa, Summers 1993 - present
Tennis, Student Coaching, Ankeny High School, Ankeny, Iowa, Spring 1994
Tennis, Private Coach, Ames and Ankeny areas, 1992 - 1994

AWARDS:

- Dean's List, 1995
- Iowa State tennis team: letter winner - 3 years; MVP - 1 year
- Nominated for the Big Eight Conference Athlete of the Year, 1995
- University Student Award for Volunteer Service, 1995
  (Volunteer service at Mary Greely Hospital, Boys' Juvenile Center, and the United Action for Youth Center)

ACTIVITIES:

Member, American Alliance for Health, Physical Education, Recreation and Dance
Student Delegate, 1994 AAHPERD National Convention
Member, Iowa Alliance for Health, Physical Education, Recreation and Dance

REFERENCES:

Career Development Center, Any City, State 12345 (101) 555-0008

J. L. DVORAK

221 College Street
Any City, State 12345
(101) 555-0009

OBJECTIVE: **Teacher: Russian Language (9-12)**

EDUCATION: The Ohio State University, Columbus, Ohio
B.S. Degree - May 1995
     Major: Russian Language
     Teaching Certificate, May 1995

The Pushkin Institute, Moscow, Russia
Exchange Program - September 1993 - June 1994

Middlebury College, Middlebury, Vermont
Summer 1993 - Russian Language

Bryn Mawr College, Bryn Mawr, Pennsylvania
Summer 1992 - Russian Language

**STUDENT
TEACHING:**   **Russian Language**, Valley High School, Columbus, 1/95-5/95
Responsibilities:
- Prepared lesson plans and objectives for levels I-IV
- Reviewed curriculum resources and created new materials
- Attended departmental meetings and support groups
- Effectively used cooperative learning strategies
- Implemented higher order thinking skills
- Involved in International Club
- Organized and created grammar explanations, games, and activities

**PRACTICUM
STUDENT:**   **English as a Second Language**, Art Middle School, Detroit, 9/94-1/95
Responsibilities:
- Assisted in all teaching responsibilities
- Provided tutorial services for students needing extra help
- Individually tutored new students

**ACTIVITIES
& AWARDS:**
- Dean's List, 1990-1995
- Ohio Critical Language Program, accepted 1992
- Member, American Association of Slavic and Eastern European Languages
- Member, Dobro Slovo, Slavic Honor Society
- Buckeye Marching and Concert Band, 1990-1992
- President, Russian Circle, 1991

**CREDENTIALS
ON FILE:**   Teacher Career Center
Any City, State 12345 (101) 555-0008

CLINT WILLIAMS

221 College Street
Any City, State 12345
(101) 555-0009

Teaching Competencies

SCIENCE
Biology
Earth Science
Environmental Studies

MATH
Algebra
Geometry
Business Math

Extracurricular Interests

Science Club Sponsor
National Honor Society

Class Sponsor
Math Bee Competition Advisor

Academic Training

University of Arkansas
Fayetteville, Arkansas

Teacher Certification
December, 1995

Science Education

Harding University
Searcy, Arkansas

B.A., 1993

Major: Science
Minor: Math

Student Teaching

H.S. Science, East High School, Fayetteville, Arkansas, fall 1995
Responsibilities included teaching units in the following classes:
- Biology I
- Advanced Biology
- Environmental Studies
- Seminar for Global Science Issues
- Physical Science

Practicum Experience

Middle School Math & Science, Lincoln Middle School, Fayetteville, spring 1994
- Assisted with teaching responsibilities in exploratory science
- Organized and led small group activities in advanced 6th grade math
- Taught a unit on rain forests and global environmental impact
- Involved in supervising computer lab for 5th grade math students

Activities & Affiliations

Co-chair, Campus Recycling Committee
Member, Arkansas Environmental Impact Coalition
Member, National Science Teachers Association
Member, Arkansas Academy of Science

Other Work Experience

Math Tutor - University Special Support Services, Fayetteville, 1995
Camp Counselor - Camp Wauwatosa, Twin Lakes, Minnesota, summers 1989-1991
Construction Worker - Department of Transportation, Little Rock, 1991-1994

Credentials available at Office of Career Planning
Any City, State 12345 (101) 555-0008

EVA JENSEN
221 College Street
Any City, State 12345
(101) 555-0009

Teaching Competencies

SPANISH
Grammar
Latin American Culture
Spanish Culture
Literature and History

JOURNALISM
News Reporting
Journalistic Writing
Photography
Broadcast Journalism

Extracurricular Interests

Soccer and Tennis Coaching
Cheerleading Sponsor

Yearbook Sponsor
Newspaper Advisor

Academic Training

Kent State University
Kent, Ohio

Teacher Certification
December, 1995

Spanish

Luther College
Decorah, Iowa

B.A., 1993
(with honors)

Major: Journalism
Major: Spanish

Student Teaching

Spanish, Roosevelt High School, Kent, Ohio, fall 1995
- Taught Spanish classes on levels I, II, III, and IV
- Prepared lesson plans and objectives using the teacher effectiveness model
- Utilized effective classroom management techniques
- Provided tutorial services for students needing additional help
- Incorporated special activities and guest speakers into curriculum
- Evaluated student progress and held regular student conferences
- Attended inservice sessions, faculty meetings and school functions

Practicum Student

Journalism, Revere High School, Richfield, Ohio, spring 1994
- Assisted with teaching responsibilities in journalism and mass communication
- Organized and led small group activities
- Developed and taught a unit on magazine writing and editing
- Involved in supervising newspaper lab

Activities & Awards

Dean's List, 1991-1993
Member, American Council for the Teaching of Foreign Languages
All-Conference tennis player and team captain, Luther College
Volunteer cheerleading sponsor, City High School, 1994-1995

Other Work Experience

Tennis Instructor - University Recreation Services, Kent, Ohio, 1994-1995
Summer Camp Counselor - Camp Foster, Arnolds Park, Iowa, summers 1989-1993
Part-time Sales Associate - Walker's Shoes, Columbus, holidays, 1988-1991

Credentials available at Career Planning & Placement
Any City, State 12345 (101) 555-0008   FAX: (101) 555-0089

MARIE LOVETINSKY

221 College Street
Any City, State 12345
(101) 555-0009

OBJECTIVE

Special Education instructor at secondary level

DEGREES

Master of Arts Degree, Special Education
Indiana State University, Terre Haute, Indiana 12/95

Bachelor of Arts Degree, Special Education
St. Mary's College, Notre Dame, Indiana 5/93

STUDENT TEACHING

High School Special Education, Johnson High School,
Terre Haute, Indiana 8/95-10/95

Middle School Special Education, Horace Mann School,
Indianapolis, Indiana 10/95-12/95

Responsibilities of the above positions included instruction of mild mental disabilities-educable in a special class with integration and moderate mental disabilities- trainable in a special self-contained class. Assessed and evaluated the individual needs of students with learning, mental and behavior disabilities. Designed and utilized IEP goals and objectives. Organized and implemented lessons in the four curricular domains with the main emphasis on concept development, language, communication, motor and self-help skills. Worked with a special education team consisting of consultant, physical therapist, occupational therapist, and speech therapist.

PRACTICA

Adaptive Physical Education Assistant, South Bend High School, South Bend, 9/92-5/93
Life Skills Training Assistant, Regional Services Office, Terre Haute, 6/93-12/93
Behavior and Emotional Disorders, North Junior High School, Bloomington, 10/94 - 12/94

RELATED ACTIVITIES

Volunteer, Special Olympics, 4 years
Organizer and volunteer, Terre Haute Special Populations Support Group
Officer, College of Education Student Service Organization

PART-TIME EXPERIENCE

Week-end manager, Active Endeavors Sports, Indianapolis, 1992-1995
Clerk, Campus Book & Supply, Terre Haute (part-time), 1994
Receptionist, St. Mary's Admissions Center, 1990-1993
(Financed college expenses through employment and loans)

PROFESSIONAL AFFILIATIONS

Indiana State Education Association
National Education Association
Council for Exceptional Children
Pi Lambda Theta
Phi Delta Kappa

CREDENTIALS

Career Planning and Placement Center
Any City, State 12345-1338 Telephone: (101) 555-0008

——— JEFFREY VANCE ———

| 221 College Street | Any City, State 12345 | (101)555-0009 |

DEGREES

Bachelor of Arts Degree, August 1995
University of Wyoming, Laramie, Wyoming
graduated with honors

Associate of Arts Degree, June 1992
Casper College, Casper, Wyoming
Dean's List

TEACHING STRENGTHS

- Speech and Drama
- Mass Communication
- Play Production
- Contemporary Literature

will direct play productions, small group and individual drama contest events

STUDENT TEACHING EXPERIENCE

Speech & English Department, Albany School District #1, Laramie, Wyoming, Fall 1994
Student taught an advanced speech course, 10th grade American Literature and Language course, upperclass Mass Communications course, and team-taught an elective speech class for juniors. Prepared educational objectives and lesson plans for three grade levels. Worked with individuals, small groups, and large groups using a variety of instructional and motivational strategies. Supervised students in the computer writing lab and initiated special after-school study reviews sessions.

Speech & Drama Volunteer, Albany School District #1, Laramie, 1994 - present.
Assisted with play productions and coached members of the speech team involved in interpretation events. Traveled to meets, chaperoned and supervised students.

Middle School Language Arts, Big Horn Middle School, Sheridan County Schools, Big Horn, Wyoming, Fall 1993. Assisted with lesson plans and progress reports. Worked with three language arts classes during novel unit. Led small group discussions and met with students on an individual basis.

RELATED EXPERIENCE

Stage assistant, costume and scenery construction, University of Wyoming Productions
Actor, Wyoming Players Repertory Company (traveling company performing statewide)
Set designer and part-time actor, Big Horn Mountains Community Theatre
Member and week-end supervisor, Gold Usher Corps, Wyoming Arts Center

PROFESSIONAL ORGANIZATIONS

Speech Communication Association
Wyoming Communication Association
National Council of Teachers of English

HONORS

Phi Beta Kappa
Dean's List
Presidential Citation
Buck Drama Scholarship

REFERENCES

Dr. Sue Pervisor	Mr. Abel Mentor	Dr. E. Val Waite
Albany School District	Albany School District	University of Wyoming
Any City, State 12345	Any City, State 12345	Any City, State 12345
(101)555-0100	(101)555-0101	(101)555-0102

VALERIE CIMMINO
221 College Street
Any City, State 12345
(101) 555-0009

EDUCATION

Secondary English - Licensure Program, Urban Teacher Development Project
Paterson Public Schools, Paterson, New Jersey, 1994-1995
The Urban Teacher Development Project awards full scholarships for study and internship opportunities leading to a professional teaching license. The Project is directed by the Paterson Public Schools in collaboration with faculty from teacher preparation institutions throughout the state who teach courses and collaborate with practitioners in the schools to supervise student teaching or internship experiences.

B.A. - Majors in English and Psychology
Glassboro State College, Glassboro, New Jersey, 1988-1992

TEACHING EXPERIENCE

Internship:
Eastside High School, Paterson, New Jersey, January-June, 1995
Taught Contemporary Writing and Basic English
Created individual reading plans for each student in Contemporary Writing, an elective course for students in grades 11 and 12 reading at or near grade level. Readings included fiction, essays, and poetry. Emphasized critical reading skills, demonstrated in oral and written responses to readings. In Basic English, required for grade 10, developed units on vocabulary building and expository writing.

Practicum Experience
Eastside and John F. Kennedy High Schools, Paterson, New Jersey, November-December, 1994
Observed classes taught by mentors, assisted with presentation of units for individual and group projects in spelling and punctuation. Worked with students individually and in small groups to improve written and oral communication.

RELATED EXPERIENCE

Counselor, Passaic County Family Court, Paterson, New Jersey, 1992-1993
Assisted victims of domestic violence in petition room filing for Orders of Protection. Provided advocacy, crisis intervention, and short-term counseling to victims of domestic violence. Provided clients with an orientation to Family Court and escorted clients to court as required. Assisted clients with direct services, such as shelters, relocation, transportation, public assistance, and referrals for long-term assistance.

Volunteer, Crisis Intervention Center, Glassboro, New Jersey, 1990-1992

REFERENCES

Dr. Sue Pervisor	Mr. Abel Mentor	Dr. E. Val Waite
Paterson Public Schools	Eastside High School	Glassboro State College
Paterson, New Jersey 07509	Paterson, New Jersey 07509	Glassboro, New Jersey 08028
(101) 555-0100	(101) 555-0101	(101) 555-0102

13

EXPERIENCED TEACHERS

JANET ALDEN
221 College Street
Any City, State 12345
(101) 555-0008

EDUCATION

M.A.   Exceptional Education - Florida State University, Tallahassee, Florida - 1993
B.S.   Economics - Bethune-Cookman College, Daytona Beach, Florida - 1986
A.S.   Computer Science - Miami-Dade Community College, Miami, Florida - 1984

TEACHING EXPERIENCE

Darnell-Cookman Counseling Center (Duval County Schools), Jacksonville, Florida, 1994-
Teach economics and computer science to students in grades 7-12 in an alternative
school setting. Teaching and advising responsibilities include:
- Create classroom environment conducive to learning and appropriate to
  maturity and interest of Center students
- Provide individualized instruction and counseling to Center students
- Supervise Center students throughout the campus and promote
  consistent behavioral control
- Design and revise economics and computer science curriculum
- Select textbooks and materials for the economics program
- Assist in placement of economics students into traditional schools
- Help other teachers with preparation of graduates from the Center
- Provide information to Center staff concerning the ability and progress
  of economics and computer science students
- Evaluate and select software in computer science and other curriculum areas
- Provide training to staff for computer assisted instruction, word processing,
  or record keeping
- Establish and maintain written and oral communication with parents

Lakewood Senior High School, Clearwater, Florida, 1986-1992
Taught economics and computer science, grades 10-12

ACTIVITIES & MEMBERSHIPS

Executive Committee, local chapter of United Action for Youth
Teacher Representative, State Advisory Committee on Adult & Community Education
Member, Florida State Secondary Economics Council
Florida Teaching Profession-National Education Association
Membership Committee, Florida Association for Women in Computer Science

References Available Upon Request

ROBIN CASE
221 College Street
Any City, State 12345
(101) 555-0009

_____ **Teaching Competencies** _____

Painting
Printmaking
Sculpture
Crafts and Ceramics
Art History

_____ **Academic Training** _____

Humboldt State University
Arcata, California

Master of Arts in Teaching - Art Education
July, 1995

Memphis State University
Memphis, Tennessee

B.S. 1993

Major: Art
Minor: African Studies

_____ **Professional Teaching Experience** _____

H.S. Art, Performing Arts High School, Los Angeles, California, 9/95-present
Teach courses in silversmithing, ceramics, watercolor and art history to advanced students. Also team-teach visual arts and humanities course for advanced placement students. Offer after-school studio sessions and class review lessons in art history. Magnet school has a diverse student body and operates year round with flexible hours. Supervise university students involved in semester-long internships and practicum assignments.

_____ **Internship Experience** _____

Middle School Art, grades 5-7, King Middle School, Los Angeles, Spring 1994

Elementary Art, grades K-3, Mountain View Academy, Nashville, Summers 1991-1992

Community Center for Visual Arts, Adult Education Division, Memphis, Fall 1991

_____ **Current Activities & Affiliations** _____

Member, Fine Arts Curriculum Development Committee, 1995-present
Council Member, South Los Angeles Art Council
Grant Writer and Recipient, Fine Arts Partnership Project
Treasurer, Black Action for Youth (BAY)
Member, National Art Teachers Association
Member, Los Angeles Academy of Fine Arts

_____ **Credentials** _____

Credentials available upon request at Career Development Center
Any City, State 12345

MICHAEL E. WALL

221 College Street, Any City, State 12345, (101) 555-0009 (home)
(101) 555-1111 (school)

OBJECTIVE:
Teacher for At-Risk Students, grades K - 8

CURRENT PROFESSIONAL EXPERIENCE:
Chapter I Teacher, Hattiesburg Public Schools, Hattiesburg, Mississippi, 1994 - present. Responsible for providing remediation in math and reading at McKenzie School. Coordinate parent involvement programs and inservice activities. Instructional strategies include extensive use of manipulatives and alternate assessment techniques. Implement NCTM standards in teaching math.

FIELD EXPERIENCES:
Elementary Math Student Teacher, Hattiesburg Public Schools, fall semester 1992.
Reading Clinic Practicum, Hattiesburg Catholic Schools, spring semester 1992.
Fourth Grade Practicum, Hattiesburg Summer School Program, summer 1991.

Responsibilities in the above field experiences included observing and assisting in all areas, working with individual students, organizing small group learning activities, tutoring remedial students and evaluating progress.

ACADEMIC TRAINING:
Master of Arts Degree-Education   University of Mississippi 1994 - present
                                          University, Mississippi

Bachelor of Science Degree-Math   University of Southern Mississippi 1989 - 1993
                                          Hattiesburg, Mississippi

GRADUATE COURSE CONCENTRATIONS:
Learning Theories   Adolescent and the Young Adult
Behavioral Principles   Construction of Evaluation Instruments
Assessment of Young Children   Interventions and Referrals

PROFESSIONAL AFFILIATIONS:
National Council of Teachers of Mathematics
National Education Association
Regional Consortium for At-Risk Students
Mississippi Council for Talented & Gifted

WORKSHOPS & SEMINARS ATTENDED:
At-Risk Students in Today's Classrooms: Symptoms and Solutions, Region 10 Consortium
    of Teachers and Social Workers, Atlanta, Georgia, March 1994.
Students at Risk: Reversing the Cycle of Educational Failure, State Education Convention,
    Mississippi Education Association, Jackson, Mississippi, February, 1993.
Conference sessions attended on topics of Whole Language, Reading Recovery, and Literacy
    at the International Reading Association Conference, San Antonio, Texas, March 1993.

REFERENCES:
Career Advising and Placement Center, Any City, State 12345
Telephone: (101) 555-0008   FAX: (101) 555-0089

TARA SAGE

221 College Street
Any City, State 12345
(101) 555-0009 (home)
(101) 555-0005 (school)

PROFESSIONAL EXPERIENCE: 16 years

Eisenhower High School, Lawton, Oklahoma, 1986-1995
Business Education Teacher, grades 10-12
Yearbook adviser
Frederick High School, Frederick, Oklahoma, 1982-1986
Business Education Teacher, grades 9-12
Yearbook and student newspaper adviser
Temple Junior-Senior High School, Temple, Oklahoma, 1979-1982
Business Education and English Teacher, grades 9-12
Student newspaper adviser, assistant basketball coach

EXPERIENCE HIGHLIGHTS:

Teaching responsibilities include courses in:

Business Calculations	Business and Contract Law
Entrepreneurship	Recordkeeping
Document Formatting	Document Production

Arranged for business internship opportunities and supervised student interns
Developed word processing short courses for faculty development series
Cooperating teacher for 11 student teachers and 8 practicum students

COMMITTEE RESPONSIBILITIES:

Faculty representative, Lawton School-Community Partnerships Study Group
Planning committee, Lawton High School Parent-Teacher Association
Computer Needs Assessment Task Force, Lawton High School
Writing Across the Curriculum Committee

PROFESSIONAL MEMBERSHIPS AND HONORS:

Nominated for Oklahoma Teacher of the Year, 1994
Outstanding Educator Award, Lawton Jaycees, 1992
Phi Delta Kappa, local chapter officer 1989-93
Oklahoma Vocational Association
Oklahoma Educational Association

SELECTED PROFESSIONAL SEMINARS, 1992-PRESENT:

Desktop Publishing for Student Journalists
Methods of Alternative Assessment
Topics in Work Force Education
Technology for Restructuring Schools
Educational Technology for "At Risk" Students

ACADEMIC BACKGROUND:

University of Oklahoma, Norman, Oklahoma
Graduate Studies - Curriculum and Instruction (Summers, 1986, 1988)
Midwestern State University, Wichita Falls, Texas
B.A. in Business Education, 1979

REFERENCES AVAILABLE UPON REQUEST AT
Placement and Teacher Certification
Any City, State 12345
(101) 555-0008 FAX: (101) 555-1118

BENJAMIN JOHNS

221 College Street
Any City, State 12345
(101) 555-0009

OBJECTIVE   Head Basketball Coach

EDUCATION   **University of New Hampshire, Durham, New Hampshire**
  M.A. Degree, Exercise Science, May, 1995
    Area of Specialization: Athletic Administration
  B.A. Degree, Physical Education and Math, 1987

COACHING
SKILLS
Develop all-around athletes both physically and mentally
Instill sportsmanship on and off the court
Thorough knowledge of basketball fundamentals, team concepts and goals
Provide excellent supervision at practices and on road trips
Coordinate all program levels - elementary leagues through varsity
Initiate and maintain communications with parents, players and administrators
Work with summer camp programs and promote athletes to college recruiters

COACHING
EXPERIENCE
Head Basketball Coach, Plymouth High School, Plymouth, New Hampshire 9/93-
Record and Accomplishments:
• **Class 3A division; 24 wins, 8 losses (1994)**
• **State qualifiers; district champions (1993,1994)**
• **Three athletes named to All-Conference Academic Team**
• **Players selected on 1st and 2nd team All-Conference**
• **Named Conference Coach of the Year (1994)**

Head Coach and Teacher, Shabazz High School, Newark, New Jersey, 1991-93

Head Coach and Athletic Director, Hayward Military Academy, Rockford, Illinois, 1988-91

Record for above positions:
• **Overall basketball record- 102 wins; 68 losses**
• **Honors include three Conference Champions, All-Conference**
  selections and sportsmanship recognition
• **Student athletes recognized by college scholarship awards**

RELATED
ACTIVITIES
Motivational speaker, state and regional camps and awards banquets
Hospice volunteer, Newark and Durham communities
Boys Club volunteer coach, Newark, summers, 1990-1992
Member, Big Brother/Big Sister Organization
President, State Special Olympics Organization, 1994
Council member, Boys Athletic Union, New Hampshire

CREDENTIALS   **Career Planning & Placement Service**
Any City, State 12345 Telephone: (101) 555-0008   FAX: (101) 555-0089

KARLA LUDKE

221 College Street   Any City, State 12345   (101) 555-0009

TEACHING COMPETENCIES
- Computer Languages
  COBOL, FORTRAN, PASCAL
- Keyboard/word processing
- Computer network administration
- Inservice computer instruction
- Hardware/software evaluation
- Programming - all levels
- Video editing/multi-media

EDUCATION

Bachelor of Science Degree, Major: Computer Science, 8/93
University of Wisconsin - Parkside, Kenosha, Wisconsin

Bachelor of Science Degree, Major: Mathematics, 1988-1992
Marshall University, Huntington, West Virginia
- Dean's List
- Vera Goode Scholarship, 1992

CLASSROOM TEACHING EXPERIENCE

H. S. Computer Science Teacher: Green Bay Public Schools, Green Bay, Wisconsin, 1994-present
Teach students at all levels of computer knowledge ranging from novice to the experienced high school programmer. Use a variety of teaching and motivational strategies to encourage students to reach their potential. Created a Computer Club, Senior Club (for advanced students) and a volunteer high school computer outreach team that visits senior citizens' centers to teach computer skills.

Computer Lab Supervisor: Lakeview Elementary, Kenosha, Wisconsin, 1992-1993
Supervised lab and instructed students from first grade through sixth grade. Designed special activities to demonstrate basic computer concepts and usage. Developed software to reinforce learning goals. Also developed and taught district-wide faculty computer mini-courses. Created a faculty computer resource center with on-going instruction for grading programs, test development, and materials design. Responsible for the repair and maintenance of equipment.

RELATED EXPERIENCE

Computer Tutor, Kenosha and Green Bay, Wisconsin, 1992-present
Summer School Computer Instructor, Green Bay Summer Program, 1994-present
Committee Chair, Green Bay Public Schools Technology Committee, 1994-present
Faculty Representative, Region 8 Technology Evaluation Committee, 1994-present

PROFESSIONAL ORGANIZATIONS

International Association for Computer Information Systems
National Council of Teachers of Mathematics
National Education Association

Credentials available at the Career Center
Any City, State 12345 Telephone: (101) 555-0008

MOLLY WARD

221 College Street	Any City, State 12345	(101) 555-0009

TEACHING EXPERIENCE:

Benton High School, St. Joseph, Missouri, 1992-present
Driver Education Teacher
Provide classroom instruction, simulation instruction, and behind-the-wheel laboratory practice on the road.

- Classroom instruction in basic and complex driving techniques and strategies, including personal and social responsibilities of drivers and inculcating safe driving habits
- Introduce driving simulator; supervise weekly simulator training for each student
- Schedule and carry out behind-the-wheel instruction to provide observation and actual driving practice for each student

Physical Education Teacher, 1988-1992

- Taught skills courses including team and individual sports and fitness activities
- Member of planning team to develop and implement coeducational Early Bird physical education classes for grades 11 and 12

COACHING & RELATED ACTIVITIES:

Women's Golf - Assistant Coach, 1989-1992
Volleyball - Assistant Coach, 1988-1992
Senior Class Adviser, 1990-present

PROFESSIONAL AFFILIATIONS:

Missouri Education Association
American Driver and Traffic Safety Education Association
American Alliance for Health, Physical Education, Recreation and Dance
Pi Lambda Theta

SPECIAL INTERESTS:

Tennis
Classic and antique automobile restoration and repair

EDUCATIONAL BACKGROUND:

Driver Education - Certification Program, 1992
Northwest Missouri State University, Maryville, Missouri

Physical Education - Bachelor's Degree, 1987
College of the Ozarks, Point Lookout, Missouri

CREDENTIALS AVAILABLE:

Education Division
Any City, State 12345
Telephone: (101) 555-0008

CARLOS SANCHEZ

221 College Street
Any City, State 12345
(101) 555-0009 (home)
(101) 545-0005 (school)

PROFESSIONAL TEACHING EXPERIENCE: 20 years
Hanover County Public Schools, Ashland, Virginia, 1981-1994
Grades 1-4 classroom teacher
Self-contained, departmentalized, cross-graded and team-teaching
organizational patterns
Goose Creek Independent Schools, Baytown, Texas, 1976-1981
Fourth grade classroom teacher
Spring Branch Independent Schools, Houston, Texas, 1974-1976
Third grade classroom teacher

EXPERIENCE HIGHLIGHTS:
Planned whole language inservice activities for primary teachers
Participated in Madeline Hunter Teacher Effectiveness Inservice Program
Designed science curriculum for first and second grade teachers
Developed science centers for the Hanover elementary schools
Implemented D.A.P. (Developmental Activities Program) in my classroom
Assisted in planning M.C.N.S. (Multi-Cultural Non-Sexist) curriculum
Supervised reading clinicians from the Virginia Reading Clinic
Trained University student teachers and practicum students
Conducted parent education classes for the district-wide P.T.A.

COMMITTEE LEADERSHIP:
Hanover County District Reading Committee
Hanover County E.L.P. (Extended Learning Program) Committee
P.T.A. faculty representative - Goose Creek and Hanover County
Baytown Task Force Co-leader - School/Community Collaboration Efforts

PROFESSIONAL MEMBERSHIPS AND HONORS:
Ashland Jaycee's Outstanding Young Educator Candidate
Apple Award - Baytown, Texas, Sponsored by KCNA-TV
Pi Lambda Theta
International Reading Association
National Council of Teachers of English
N.E.A., V.S.E.A., S.E.A., and H.C.E.A.

ACADEMIC BACKGROUND:
Mary Washington College, Fredricksburg, Virginia
Graduate Studies - Curriculum and Instruction, 1988-present
Southwest Texas State University, San Marcos, Texas
B.A. in Elementary Education, 1974
Austin Community College, Austin, Texas
A.A. in Liberal Arts, 1972

RECENT PROFESSIONAL SEMINARS, 1990-present:
National Research Symposium on Talent Development, Notre Dame University
Mastery Teaching Project, Old Dominion University
Cooperative Learning, University of Richmond
Whole Language, North Carolina State University
Writing Workshops for Elementary Teachers, Wake Forest University

REFERENCES AVAILABLE UPON REQUEST AT
Placement and Teacher Certification
Any City, State 12345
(101) 555-0008 FAX: (101) 555-1118

NICOLE LOUVAR

221 College Street
Any City, State 12345
(101) 555-0009

OBJECTIVE

Elementary Departmentalized Math

EDUCATIONAL BACKGROUND

University of Arkansas - Little Rock Little Rock, Arkansas	1990-1993	B.S. Elementary Education *Areas of Specialization:* Mathematics and Science
Phillips Junior College New Orleans, Louisiana	1988-1990	L.P.N. Nursing

MATHEMATICS AND SCIENCE - COURSES OF INTEREST

Calculus I & II	Organic Chemistry I & II
Linear Algebra	Anatomy and Physiology
Computing with Fortran	Physics
Statistics	Microbiology

TEACHING EXPERIENCE

Stowe Elementary School, Fort Worth Independent School District, Fort Worth, Texas, August, 1993 - present
<u>Classroom Teacher - Grade 2 and Departmentalized Math</u>
Taught in both a self-contained and departmentalized classroom setting; utilized the methods of The Writing Process, whole language, and the integrated language arts; applied a variety of math problem solving techniques; field-tested new math curriculum. Activities included: First Grade Math Bee Coordinator, Social Committee Chairperson, Campus Coordinating Committee Member, Fort Worth Teachers' and Community Advocacy Committee Representative.

Amon Carter Jr. YMCA, Fort Worth, Texas, Summer 1993
<u>Coordinator and Instructor</u> - "Live and Learn," a program for middle school students identified as at-risk. Designed and presented life-skill lessons through the use of group discussions, guest speakers, field trips, and active participation. Actively involved business leaders in life-skill program.

Eisenhower Elementary School, Little Rock School District, Little Rock, Arkansas, Spring 1991
<u>Student Teacher - Grade 4</u>
Developed and taught poetry unit; instructed and supervised the use of the computer; worked with individuals in math; introduced and helped maintain daily journal writing; prepared and participated in Valentine's Week and Hundredth Day activities; helped organize an all-school environmental awareness project.

Hoover Elementary School, Fayetteville School District, Fayetteville, Arkansas, Fall 1989
<u>Practicum Teacher - Grade 6</u>
Experience focused primarily on science instruction. Developed and taught science lessons; assisted with computer activities and individual work in math and science.

PROFESSIONAL DEVELOPMENT COURSES

Classroom Management	Peer Coaching	Improving Student Writing
Quest	NASA Math	Newspapers in Education

CREDENTIALS at Teacher Career Center
Any City, State 12345 Telephone: (101) 555-0008

FRANK VINCENT

221 College Street
Any City, State 12345
(101) 555-0009

TEACHING INTERESTS AND METHODS

Writing Workshops
Computer Writing Lab
Career Education
Technology Education

Higher Order Thinking Skills
Authentic Assessment
Cooperative Learning
Mastery Learning

CLASSROOM EXPERIENCE

Pekin Community High School, Pekin, Illinois, 1991 - present
<u>English and journalism teacher, grades 9-12</u>
Drama director
Newspaper and newsletter advisor

EXPERIENCE HIGHLIGHTS

- Created new language arts curriculum for grades 9 and 10
- Planned whole language programs
- Designed an advanced composition course utilizing Bloom's Taxonomy
- Implemented career education and life skills through writing assignments
- Infused multi-cultural, non-sexist literature in the curriculum
- Modified course work to involve higher order thinking skills
- Developed a program to increase voluntary reading
- Supervised a variety of cooperative learning projects in the classroom
- Directed two drama productions each school year
- Produced a monthly school newsletter using the Macintosh computer
- Served as a member of the At-Risk Committee

PROFESSIONAL AFFILIATIONS

National Council of Teachers of English
Illinois Council of Teachers of English
National Education Association
Illinois State Education Association

EDUCATIONAL BACKGROUND

University of Illinois at Urbana-Champaign, Champaign, Illinois
Bachelor of Arts Degree, May, 1991
Majors: English and Journalism
Minor: Drama

CREDENTIALS

Education Placement Office, Any City, State 12345
Telephone: (101) 555-0008 FAX: (101) 555-0089

CHARLES CASLIN

221 College Street
Any City, State 12345
(101) 555-0009 (home)
(101) 545-0005 (school)

PROFESSIONAL TEACHING EXPERIENCE: 8 years

Kansas City Public Schools, Kansas City, Missouri, 1992-present
German, Grades 1-4 (1992-1993); Grades 9-12 (currently)

San Antonio Independent Schools, San Antonio, Texas, 1990-1992
German, Middle School grades, 5-7

Saint Louis Independent Schools, St. Louis, Missouri, 1986-1989
Bilingual, Transitional Elementary grades, 4-6

EXPERIENCE HIGHLIGHTS:

Instructed students at all levels in German in traditional and transitional settings
Participated in Bilingual Teacher Intensive Training Program
Designed German curriculum for fourth through sixth grade classes
Developed bilingual learning centers for middle school students
Implemented positive classroom management strategies in all my classrooms
Co-directed the Multi-Cultural Non-Sexist Curriculum Project
Created a bilingual parent-student newsletter to improve parent involvement

COMMITTEE LEADERSHIP:

District Committee for Magnet Schools
Co-chair, Elementary German Curriculum Revision Project
Faculty Representative to Superintendent's Roundtable
Kansas City Bilingual Consortium

PROFESSIONAL MEMBERSHIPS:

American Association of Teachers of German
Missouri Association of Teachers of German
American Federation of Teachers
International German Student Society

ACADEMIC BACKGROUND:

University of Missouri-Kansas City, Kansas City, Missouri
    Graduate Studies - ESL and Bilingual Education, 1992-present
Black Hills State University, Spearfish, South Dakota
    B.A. German and Elementary Education, 1985

RECENT PROFESSIONAL SEMINARS, 1990-present:
Midwest Regional Students-At-Risk Symposium, Washington University
Missouri Native Language Project, University Of Missouri-Columbia
Cooperative Learning, University of Northern Iowa
Language Immersion Experiment, North Dakota State University
Language Learning Centers for Elementary Teachers, University of Chicago

REFERENCES AVAILABLE UPON REQUEST AT
Placement and Teacher Certification
Any City, State 12345
(101) 555-0008 FAX: (101) 555-1118

TERRY POINTER
221 College Street
Any City, State 12345
(101) 555-0008

EDUCATION

M.A. - Gifted Education - Eastern Kentucky University, Richmond, Kentucky - 1991

Certification Program - Elementary Education - Ohio University, Athens, Ohio - 1986

B.A. - Music - Valparaiso University, Valparaiso, Indiana - 1984

TEACHING EXPERIENCE

Teacher, Extended Learning Program - Marion City School District, Marion, Ohio, 1993-
  Work with ELP Teacher Committees to schedule and coordinate school visits by
    speakers and visiting artists and field experiences for large and small
    groups of elementary students.
  Facilitate enrichment experiences for students interested in more indepth exploration
    of a topic.
  Develop and conduct enrichment lessons and units, with particular emphasis on music
    and performing arts.
  Work directly with elementary students as an enrichment facilitator.
  Conduct student assessment, and provide inservice for educators and parents.
  Participate in Extended Learning Program Advisory Committee.

Teacher, Grades 4-6, Indian Mound Elementary School, Marion, Ohio, 1986-1992
  Taught reading, language arts, mathematics, and science in grade 4; music in grades
  4-6 in semi-departmentalized setting.

RECENT CONFERENCES ATTENDED

"Identification of Gifted Minority Students," Southern Illinois University, Carbondale,
Illinois, 1994

"Gender Roles: Impact on Giftedness," Ohio University, Athens, Ohio, 1993

Henry B. & Jocelyn Wallace National Research Symposium on Talent Development, Connie
Belin National Center for Gifted Education, The University of Iowa, Iowa City, Iowa, 1993

REFERENCES

Educational Career Services
Any City, State 12345
Telephone: (101) 555-0008   FAX: (101) 555-0089

CRAIG OVERLAND

221 College Street
Any City, State 12345
(101) 555-0009

————— Teaching Interests —————

MATHEMATICS

Pre-Algebra, Algebra, Advanced Algebra
Geometry, Trigonometry & Finite Mathematics
Pre-Calculus, Calculus

————— Professional Teaching Experience —————

Mathematics, Newnan High School, Newnan, Georgia, 9/91-present
Teach one section of Advanced Placement Mathematics, two sections of Geometry, and two sections of
Advanced Algebra; encourage students to use scientific calculators and assist with their use; incorporate
significant amounts of algebra in Geometry courses, and introduced proofs in a flow-chart format.

College Algebra Instructor, Newnan Center of West Georgia College, 1995
As adjunct faculty member, taught two semesters of Beginning Algebra and two semesters of Intermediate
Algebra to adult college students enrolled in evening classes through the Division of Continuing Education of
West Georgia College.
Beginning Algebra course encompassed material similar to a first-year high school Algebra course including
real numbers, linear equations, factoring, exponents, and simple graphing.
Intermediate Algebra covered material comparable to a second-year high school Algebra course, including
functions and graphing, polynomials, solving inequalities, second degree equations, systems of equations,
and logarithms.

————— Current Activities & Affiliations —————

Co-chair, Newnan High School Curriculum Review Committee
Board member, Georgia Council of Teachers of Mathematics (GCTM)
Member, National Council of Teachers of Mathematics
Awarded GCTM Grant for Advanced Placement Teacher Training
Founding Member, Metropolitan Area Mathematics Club

————— Academic Training —————

University of Georgia Athens, Georgia	M.A., 1991	Mathematics Education
Augusta College Augusta, Georgia	B.S., 1984	Major: Mathematics Minor: Computer Science

————— Credentials —————

Office of Career Planning
Any City, State 12345 (101) 555-0008

MARGO BURKHART

221 College Street, Any City, State 12345 (101) 555-0008

OBJECTIVE

Teacher of Advanced Placement Mathematics and Computer Science

TEACHING EXPERIENCE

1989- present Tara High School, Baton Rouge, Louisiana
Teach Advanced Algebra, Geometry, and Computer Programming
- Project leader for grant that resulted in funding to provide each math student with a scientific calculator
- Organized peer tutoring groups for mathematics
- Founded and sponsor student mathematics club
- Chair faculty software evaluation committee

1986-1988 Tulane University, New Orleans, Louisiana
Teaching Assistant, Mathematics Department
- Taught Introduction to Calculus (three sections)
- Assisted in Undergraduate Mathematics Laboratory
- Tutored undergraduate students in calculus

1984-1986 Lawless High School, New Orleans, Louisiana
High School Mathematics Teacher
- Taught Algebra and Geometry
- Sponsored Academic Decathlon

EDUCATION

University of Texas, Austin, Texas - Advanced Placement Summer Workshop, 1990

Tulane University, New Orleans, Louisiana - M.S. Mathematics, 1988

Xavier University of Louisiana, New Orleans - B.S. Mathematics, 1984
B.S. Computer Science, 1983

PROFESSIONAL ASSOCIATIONS

National Council of Teachers of Mathematics
Louisiana Association of Teachers of Mathematics
Association for Women in Mathematics
Louisiana Association of Educators

REFERENCES

Career Planning and Placement Center
Any City, State 12345
Telephone: (101) 555-0008

SOFIA WESTIN

221 College Street
Any City, State 12345
(101) 555-0009 (home)
(101) 545-0005 (school)

PROFESSIONAL TEACHING EXPERIENCE: 7 years

Mayville-Portland School District, Mayville, North Dakota, 1991-present
Instrumental Music Teacher and Department Chair, Mayville High School

Devils Lake School District 1, Devils Lake, North Dakota, 1989-1990
Instrumental and Vocal Teacher, Central Junior Senior High School

Mustang Independent School District, Mustang, Oklahoma, 1986-1989
Instrumental Music Teacher, Mustang High School

EXPERIENCE HIGHLIGHTS:

Organized and hosted the first state-wide junior high honor band festival
Developed creative and fresh marching band scores for three marching bands
Received highest honors at the North Dakoka State Marching Band Contest
Evaluated curriculum for three districts and revived programs with new ideas
Chosen as the top state jazz band in North Dakota, 1994

CURRENT LEADERSHIP:

President, State Bandmasters Association
Chair, Plains Music Consortium for Instrumental Teachers
Faculty Liaison, Fine Arts Committee for Music Improvement in North Dakota
State Delegate, National Education Association Convention, Los Angeles

PROFESSIONAL MEMBERSHIPS:

Percussive Arts Society
American Bandmasters Association
American School Band Directors' Association
National Education Association

ACADEMIC BACKGROUND:

Mayville State University, Mayville, North Dakota
M.A. Performance and Conducting, 1993
University of North Dakota, Grand Forks, North Dakota
B.M. Instrumental Music Education   Specialty: Percussion

HONORS AND ACTIVITIES:

Selected Outstanding Music Teacher of the Year, North Dakota, 1994
Awarded Outstanding Graduate Student in Music Education, 1992
Member, North Dakota Symphony Orchestra
Percussion Ensemble, Symphony Orchestra, Marching Band
Original scores published by Northwestern Music Publishers, Seattle

REFERENCES AVAILABLE UPON REQUEST AT
Career Planning & Placement Center
Any City, State 12345
(101) 555-0008 FAX: (101) 555-1118

BRUCE O'NEILL

221 College Street
Any City, State 12345
(101) 555-0009

OBJECTIVE   Elementary General Music (K-6)

SPECIALIZED SKILLS
Aesthetic education studies and concepts
Synthesizer and audio technology
Classroom use of keyboards and guitar
Composer and creative producer

CLASSROOM EXPERIENCE

Elementary General Music - 6 years
Manhattan Public Schools, Manhattan, Kansas, 1988 - present

Middle School Instrumental Music - 3 years
St. John's Academy, Kansas City, Kansas, 1985 - 1988

<u>School district committee service in above positions includes</u>:
- NCA Evaluation team member for Shawnee Mission Schools, 1995
- Curriculum development team member and writer for K-3 music, 1994 -
- Chair, Fine Arts Committee, 1990 - 1992
- Member, Manhattan District-wide Computer Committee, 1988 - 1990
- Faculty Representative, Community & School Advisory Board, 1986 - 1988

LEADERSHIP & ACTIVITIES
Elected President, Kansas Music Educators Council
Received Educator-of-the-Year Award, Kansas Education Association
Supervised university student teachers and spoke to methods classes
Wrote and directed two middle school musicals
Produced several highly successful high school musicals
Published: "Electronics in Music Classrooms," <u>Music Educator's Journal</u>,
    Vol 12, p. 39-43, 1992
Director, Manhattan Boy's Choir (performed in Austria, Italy and several U.S. cities)

AFFILIATIONS
Music Educators National Conference
Kansas Music Educators Association
National Education Association

EDUCATION
Kansas State University, Manhattan, Kansas
 M.A. Degree - May, 1990
 Music Education and Theory

Bowdoin College, Brunswick, Maine
 B.M. Degree - August 1985
 Music Education Emphasis: Trumpet

HONORS
Outstanding Performer Award, Bowdoin College
Ken March Award for Talented Music Major, Bowdoin College
First Chair, Bowdoin College Concert Band
Composition Award and Dean's Recognition Award, Kansas State University

CREDENTIALS   Career Development Office, Any City, State 12345 (101) 555-0008

NINA CHAVEZ-HOUSTON

221 College Street   Any City, State 12345   (101) 555-0008

EDUCATION

College of Santa Fe, Santa Fe, New Mexico, 1987-1990
B.S. - Elementary Education
Emphasis: Early Childhood Education
Minor: Sociology

Aims Community College, Greeley, Colorado, 1985-1987
A.A. - Child Development

PROFESSIONAL EXPERIENCE

Parent Involvement Teacher
Trinidad School District, Trinidad, Colorado, 1992-present
Promote effective involvement of parents of pre-school children in
    program services and child development
Serve as liaison with Migrant Child and Family Service
Make referrals to agencies addressing health, nutrition, social service, or
    other needs of migrant children
Plan and conduct parenting classes in English and Spanish for school-age
    parents of migrant children

RELATED EXPERIENCE

Child Welfare Case Aide
Kit Carson County Social Services, Burlington, Colorado, 1990-1992
Assisted caseworkers in providing assistance to children of migrant
families; handled routine client inquiries and made referrals to
caseworker or other agencies; translated Spanish/English as required.

REFERENCES

Dr. Sue Pervisor   Abel Mentor
Trinidad School District   College of Santa Fe
Any City, State 12345   Any City, State 12345
Telephone: (101) 555-0100   Telephone: (101) 555-0101

Dr. E. Val Waite
Kit Carson County Social Services
Any City, State 12345
Telephone: (101) 555-0102

ANDREW MCDONALD
221 College Street
Any City, State 12345
(101) 555-0009

Teaching Competencies

CLASSROOM
Physical Education
Health Education
General Science

COACHING
Wrestling
Track
Summer Baseball

Extracurricular Interests

Booster Club Coordinator
Fund-raising Organizer

Weight Lifting Club Sponsor
Intramural Sponsor

Classroom Teaching

H.S. Physical Education and Health, East Bay High School, Seattle, Washington, January, 1995 -
Responsibilities include teaching units in the following areas:
- Health Awareness Issues
- Physical Education, all grade levels
- Co-ed Weight Lifting
- Physical Fitness and Weight Control
- Seminar on AIDS

Practicum Experience

Geriatric Leisure Activities, Bellevue Community Center, Bellevue, Washington, spring 1993
- Assisted with all leisure activities involving senior citizens
- Organized and led small group activities in exercising and swimming
- Involved in daily contact with volunteers, administrators and senior citizens

Activities & Affiliations

Baseball Coach, East Bay High School, 1995 - present
Wrestling Coach, Spokane Junior League, 1990-1993
All-Conference Selection, Wrestling, Gonzaga University, 1992
Baseball Coach, Spokane Summer Recreation League, 1990-92
Fundraiser and Benefit Chair, Washington Heart Association

Other Work Experience

Coach and Summer Recreation Assistant Director - Seattle North YMCA, 1994-present
Camp Counselor - Camp East Bay, Vancouver, Washington, summers 1990-1993

Academic Training

Gonzaga University
Spokane, Washington

Bachelor of Science Degree
May, 1993

Major: Leisure Studies
Minor: Health Education

Credentials available at Center for Career Services
Any City, State 12345 (101) 555-0008

MARGARET WISNIEWSKI
221 College Street
Any City, State 12345
(101) 555-0009

─────────────── **Teaching Competencies** ───────────────

SCIENCE
Chemistry
Biology
Earth Science
Environmental Studies

─────────────── **Professional Teaching Experience** ───────────────

High School Science, Technology & Science High School, Wichita, Kansas, 9/95-present

Teach upper-level science courses in chemistry, biology and environmental studies. Magnet school has a multicultural student body operating as an all-year-round school with flexible hours. Teach vocational science courses preparing students for the world of work and teach advanced studies to college-bound students. Supervise students participating in internships with local businesses.

─────────────── **Internship Experience** ───────────────

Middle School Science, Westfield Middle School, Wichita, Kansas, spring 1994

High School Chemistry, Cambridge Academy, Cambridge, Massachusetts, summer 1992

Outward Bound-Oregon, Wilderness Program, Greenwich, Connecticut, 1991

─────────────── **Academic Training** ───────────────

Wichita State University Wichita, Kansas	Master of Arts in Teaching December, 1995	Science
Boston University Boston, Massachusetts	B.S., 1993	Major: Biology Minor: Chemistry

─────────────── **Current Activities & Affiliations** ───────────────

Chair, Technology Department, 1995 - present
Council Member, Superintendent's Roundtable, 1995 - present
Grant recipient, Environmental Studies Collaboration Project,
(project includes five districts and Wichita State, 1994 - present)
Member, Collegiate Curriculum Review Committee, 1993
President, State Sierra Club, 1993 - 1994
Member, National Science Teachers Association
Member, Academy of Science

─────────────── **Credentials** ───────────────

Credentials available at Office of Career Planning
Any City, State 12345 (101) 555-0008

DANIEL KANE

PRESENT ADDRESS
221 College Street
Any City, State 12345
(101) 555-0009

SCHOOL ADDRESS
30 Royal Avenue
Mytown, State 23456
(909) 333-0003

OBJECTIVE
Social Studies Instructor
Co-curricular Sponsor
Athletic Coach

TEACHING SKILLS and INTERESTS
• Challenge and motivate students in a multicultural setting
• Utilize effective classroom management and discipline strategies
• Create and implement interdisciplinary materials
• Implement innovative instructional plans (community resources, case studies, simulations, field trips, computer instruction)
• Participate actively in team instructional and co-curricular planning

ACADEMIC BACKGROUND
University of Missouri-Columbia, Columbia, Missouri
Graduate Studies, College of Education, 1992 - present
Bachelor of Arts Degree, 1987
Major: Social Studies Education Emphasis: Geography
   Dean's List, University Honors Program
   Daren Goode Undergraduate Geography Scholarship

CLASSROOM TEACHING EXPERIENCE
Hickman Senior High School, Columbia, Missouri   *1991 - 1993*
Pruitt Military Academy, St. Louis, Missouri   *1987 - 1991*
Summer Learning Program, St. Louis, Missouri   *Summer 1991*

Responsibilities during the above teaching positions included:
• Taught various courses including Geography, Latin American Studies, World Cultures, Area Studies and American History
• Participated in daily team meetings to plan and implement interdisciplinary teaching units
• Worked with English, Science and Art teachers in designing curricula for Latin American interdisciplinary materials
• Developed prototype for district-wide portfolio for student academic assessment
• Encouraged parents to volunteer and participate in their student's learning and in school functions
• Helped parents organize volunteer action groups

COACHING EXPERIENCE
Cross Country Head Coach, Hickman High School, 1991 - 1993
Track and Cross Country Head Coach, Pruitt Academy, 1987 - 1991
Boys Club Track Volunteer Coach, St Louis, 1989 - 1990
City Track Club Sprint Coach, St. Louis, 1987 - 1990
   (Three Conference Championships, Cross Country State Title, numerous all-conference selections, Conference Coach of-the-Year Award-1992, three sprinters invited to Olympic trials)

DANIEL KANE
page 2

CO-CURRICULAR EXPERIENCES
Academic Decathlon Sponsor, 4 years
National Geography Bee Coach, 2 years
Student Senate Advisor, 4 years
International Club Sponsor, 2 years
History Fair Sponsor, 3 years
Junior Historian Club Advisor, 1 year
National Honor Society Advisor, 4 years

COMMITTEE and WORKSHOP ACTIVITIES
• Interdisciplinary Committee Chair, Hickman High School, 1993
• Social Studies Curriculum Review Committee Member, Columbia Schools, 1992
• Site-based Decision Making Committee member, Hickman High School, 1992
• Workshop Leader, New Staff Inservice-training, St. Louis, 1990 - 1991
• NCA Evaluation Team Member, Blue Springs High Schools, 1991 and 1992

MEMBERSHIPS and LICENSURE
National Council for Social Studies
American Federation of Teachers
State Social Studies Council
Teaching certificates-Missouri and Kansas
Coaching endorsements-Missouri, Kansas, Iowa

COMMUNITY ACTIVITIES
Fundraiser, Greater Columbia area for Disabled
Board member and Volunteer, Columbia United Way
Media Marathon Volunteer, American Heart Association
Troop Leader, Brownie Scout Troop #121

ATHLETIC RECOGNITION
• All-American Selection in track
• Captain and Most Valuable Player
• Outstanding Leadership Award
• First team All-Conference
• MVP, Drake Relays
• Academic All-Big Eight

PLACEMENT FILE
Credentials at Career Planning & Placement
Any City, State 12345 (101) 555-0008 FAX: (101) 555-0089

JULIET STRAUSS
221 College Street
Any City, State 12345
(101) 555-1111

DEGREES

M.A. Special Education, Texas Woman's University, Denton, Texas June 1992
Thesis: Community Mobility of Emotionally Disturbed Teenagers in Group Home Settings
   Adviser: Dr. Will B. Prof, Department Chair
B.A. Special Education   Emphasis: Behavior Disorders May 1984

CLASSROOM EXPERIENCE

Special Education Teacher, grades 10 - 12, Special Services Alternative Center, Dallas, Texas, August 1993 - present. Case manager for emotionally and behaviorally disturbed students removed from local high school programs. Responsibilities include interfacing with outside referral agencies on behalf of students, coordinating the instructional programs, developing appropriate Individual Education Plans, and designing and monitoring specialized behavior management programs.

Special Education Teacher, grades 7 and 8, Connally Independent School District, Waco, Texas, 1990 - 1992. Self-contained with integration classroom for emotionally disturbed students. Major teaching responsibilities included reading, mathematics, and social studies. Implemented initial stages of the special education immersion program placing students in regular academic classrooms.

Special Education Teacher, grades 5 - 12, North Texas Residential Care Center, Dallas, Texas, 1986 - 1990. Semi-residential placement center for emotionally disturbed students ages 10 to 18. Teaching responsibilities included all curricular areas. Assisted psychologist in assessment of students with behavioral or emotional problems.

UNIVERSITY ASSISTANTSHIP

Supervisor of Student Teachers, Texas Woman's University, Denton, Texas, 1992 - 1993.
Supervised undergraduate special education student teachers in three school districts. Provided guidance to students regarding their instructional techniques and overall classroom performances during semester-long internship experience.

RELATED WORK EXPERIENCE

Systems Unlimited Inc., Dallas, Texas, 1984 - 1986
   Teacher for Summer Program, 1984 - 1986
   Planned activities for 12 - 16 year old behavior disorder students.
   Family and Child Trainer, 1985 - 1986
   Provided 24 hour care for three severe/profound girls ages four to six.
   Direct Care Staff, 1984 - 1985
   Charged with the complete care of five severe/profound disabled teenagers
   in a group home setting.

PRESENTATIONS

"Evaluation of Video Feedback as a Training Procedure for BD Students." Poster presentation
   at the Convention for the Association for Behavior Analysis, Phoenix, Arizona, April 1994.
"Alternative Settings for Success." Presentation at the Texas Special Education Conference, San
   Antonio, Texas, November 1993.
"Community Mobility and Special Populations." Breakout session facilitator, Special Education
   Regional Convention, Corpus Christi, Texas, May 1992.

References provided upon request.

DAVID WONG
221 College Street
Any City, State 12345
(101) 555-0009

TEACHING INTERESTS

Communication Technology
Posters, Ads, Photography
Video Technology
Cooperative Group Skills
Verbal and Written Skills

Design Technology
Sketching
Drafting Skills
Design Process: Problem-Solving
Computer Assisted Design (CAD)

TEACHING EXPERIENCE

Fort Scott Senior High School, Fort Scott, Kansas 1986 - present
   Technology Education Teacher, grades 10-12
      Co-advisor, school yearbook and student government
      Senior class advisor
Fort Scott Community College, Fort Scott, Kansas, 1990 - present
   Instructor, responsible for teaching one or two courses per year, including foundations of design, drawing, lettering, commercial design, and visual communication
Manhattan USD 383, Manhattan, Kansas, 1985-86
   Substitute teacher in technology, science, mathematics, and industrial arts at Manhattan Senior High and Middle School

PROFESSIONAL AFFILIATIONS

Kansas Vocational Association
Mid-America Association for Computers in Education
Kansas Council on Vocational Education

EDUCATION

Emporia State University, Emporia, Kansas, Summer, 1986 - present
   24 graduate hours in vocational and technical education, art, and adult and continuing education
Alaska Pacific University, Anchorage, Alaska, 1981-1985
   Technology Education, Bachelor of Science Degree, 1991

CREDENTIALS

Career Development & Placement Services, Any City, State 12345
   Telephone: (101) 555-0008 FAX: (101) 555-0089

14

SPECIAL SERVICES

——— OLIVIA JORDAN ———

| 221 College Street | Any City, State 12345 | (101) 555-0009 |

ACADEMIC BACKGROUND

| Oregon State University | B.S. Degree | Major: Athletic Training |
| Corvallis, Oregon | 1995 | Minor: Biology |

| Evergreen State College | Summer | Student Trainer Clinic |
| Olympia, Washington | 1995 | |

COURSES OF INTEREST

Medical Supervision of Athletics
Counseling for Related Professions
Diagnostic Techniques and Treatment of
    Athletic Injuries

Biomechanics of Human Motion
Contemporary Nutrition
Clinical Sciences in Athletic Training
Introduction to Computing with FORTRAN

STUDENT TRAINING EXPERIENCES

Athletic Trainer Internship, Capital High School, Olympia, Washington, Fall, 1995
    Responsibilities included triage coverage of football team consisting of 70 athletes in
    grades 10 through 12. Experience gained in injury rehabilitation programs, first-aid
    applications, fluid replacement, practice supervision, and facility maintenance.

Student Trainer, Oregon State University, Corvallis, Oregon, 1995
    Responsibilities as a student trainer for various men's and women's sports; involved in all
    aspects of the college's training program including diagnosis, treatment, and rehabilitation.

TEAM EXPERIENCE

Volleyball	Training Camp	1995
	Conference Tournament	1994
	Conference Finals	1993
	Home Games	1993
Tennis	Team Coverage and Oregon Invitational Meet	1994
Football	Team Coverage	1994
	Spring Scrimmage	1993
Soccer	Home Games and Regional Finals	1993

REHABILITATION EXPERIENCE

Rehabilitation program involved treatment strategies, evaluation consultations, and follow-up treatment for various sports. Observed three major surgical procedures for knee, shoulder, and ankle injuries.

Special personal skills include swimmers' shoulder problems, ACL knee reconstruction, joint mobilization, and post-operative rehabilitation.

RELATED SUMMER WORK EXPERIENCES

Tennis	Oregon State University Summer Camps	1994
Basketball	Oregon High School Basketball Camps	1992-93
Coach	Corvallis City Softball League	1990-93
Umpire	Lincoln High School Junior League	1988-90
Lifeguard	Corvallis Parks & Recreation Program	1986-90

DISTINCTIONS

Oregon State University's Dean's List, 1995
Outstanding Clinical and Academic Student Trainer Award, 1995
Olympia Club Scholarship, 1992
All-State High School Swimmer, 1991 and 1992

CERTIFICATION AND MEMBERSHIPS

American Red Cross First Aid Certificate
American Heart Association CPR
National Athletic Trainers Association, Student Member
Oregon Athletic Trainers Society, Member

CREDENTIALS

Career Planning and Placement Center
Any City, State 12345 (101) 555-0008

LOIS HATHAWAY

221 College Street   Any City, State 12345   (101) 555-0009

ACADEMIC BACKGROUND

Colorado State University   M.S.   Audiology
Fort Collins, Colorado   1995

University of Colorado   B.S.   Speech & Hearing
Boulder, Colorado   1993

COURSE HIGHLIGHTS

Pediatric Audiology   **Tests and Measurements**
Remedial Methods in Speech and Hearing   **Clinical Audiology**
Rehabilitative Audiology   **Hearing Aids I, II**

PRACTICUM EXPERIENCES

Northeast Board of Cooperative Educational Services, Longmont, Colorado, January-May, 1995
    Participated in identification program for hearing disorders, including kindergarten
    screening. Select and implement therapy strategies for modifying communicative
    behavior of students with hearing problems. Participated in conferences with teachers
    and parents to foster communication and to develop appropriate intervention strategies.
Colorado School for the Deaf and the Blind, Colorado Springs, Colorado, October-December, 1994
    Observe and assist with evaluation of children for hearing impairment, confer with
    physicians, parents and technicians regarding hearing aids, or other appropriate treatment
    and therapy.

RELATED EMPLOYMENT

Colorado Lions Camp, Woodland Park, Colorado - Summers, 1991-1993
    Residential counselor for hearing-impaired campers, ages 8-16; assist with recreational
    activities including backpacking, hiking, overnight camping, and arts and crafts.

MEMBERSHIPS & ACTIVITIES

American Speech and Hearing Association
Volunteer, Zebulon Pike Youth Services Center, Colorado Springs
Secretary, Iowa Audiology Students' Association

CREDENTIALS

Educational Placement Office
Any City, State 12345 (101) 555-0008

IVY JONES

221 College Street
Any City, State 12345
(101) 555-0009

OBJECTIVE   Counselor: Elementary (K-6) or Secondary (7-12)

EDUCATION   University of Nevada - Reno
  M.A. Degree - May, 1995
    Counseling and Human Development
    Area of Specialization: School Counseling
  B.A. Degree - August, 1993
    Home Economics Education and Spanish

COUNSELING SKILLS
Provide individual counseling
Facilitate small group counseling sessions
Conduct classroom guidance activities
Consult with parents, teachers and community specialists
Coordinate outreach services to families
Use bilingual counseling skills (Spanish)

COUNSELING EXPERIENCE

Middle School Counselor, 4th - 7th grades, Lake Tahoe School, 9/95-present

Responsibilities:
• Create a positive and supportive school counseling climate
• Initiate conflict management action groups for students
• Organize before school sessions for new students
• Implement student-centered lunch seminars on topics dealing
    with coping skills, grief & loss, study habits and AIDS
• Incorporate peer counseling skills into 6th grade curriculum
• Use a variety of intervention techniques for at-risk students
• Provide resource materials for students exploring careers
• Initiate and conduct parent-teacher-counselor conferences at student's home

7-12 grades Counseling Internship, Mountain High School, 2/94-4/94

Responsibilities:
• Administered and scored individualized achievement tests and
    assisted students in preparation for college admissions examinations
• Met with students on a regular basis to discuss career options
• Designed and maintained progress charts for students on suspension
• Conducted a student needs analysis survey of all high school grades
• Attended Student Study Team meetings and staffings for students
    on school suspension or parole

RELATED ACTIVITIES
Adviser to Board of Directors, Domestic Violence Abuse Shelter, 1994-present
Volunteer, Hispanic Community Center, 1994-present
Member, American Counseling Association
President, Reno Youth Shelter Foundation, 1992

CREDENTIALS   Career Development and Advising Office
Any City, State 12345 (101) 555-0008 FAX: (101) 555-0089

MARTIN SYDLOSKI

221 College Street
Any City, State 12345
(101) 555-0009

COUNSELING COMPETENCIES

Crisis Intervention
Multicultural Counseling
Conflict Management

Group & Individual Therapy
Chemical & Substance Abuse
Self-esteem & Relationship Skills

COUNSELING EXPERIENCE

King High School and Alternative Center, Detroit Public Schools, 1993 - present
Crisis Counselor and Substance Abuse Specialist

Riverside Intermediate School, Dearborn Heights Public Schools, 1991 - 1993
Middle School Counselor

Youth Emergency Shelter, Detroit, Michigan, Summers, 1991 - present
Crisis Intervention Counselor and Youth Advocate

Responsibilities in the above positions included:
- Implementation of crisis intervention counseling programs and activities at all levels
- Collaboration with mental health agencies and community resources to provide services for students and families
- Coordination with state and local programs in chemical abuse projects
- Development of various programs to assist students with personal and family crises

CLASSROOM EXPERIENCE

Ford High School, Detroit Public Schools, 1987 - 1990
Journalism teacher, junior and senior division
Student Affirmative Action Liaison; Yearbook Video Advisor

East Catholic High School, Detroit, Michigan, 1984 - 1987
Journalism, Drama and Debate teacher, grades 9-12
Community Action Club Advisor; Peer Tutoring Coordinator

PROFESSIONAL AFFILIATIONS

National Counselor Certification Board
Association for Multicultural Counseling and Development
American Association for Counseling and Development
Michigan Association for Counseling and Development
National Education Association and Michigan State Education Association

EDUCATIONAL BACKGROUND

Wayne State University, Detroit, Michigan
Bachelor of Arts Degree, 1988 Major: Journalism; Minor: African Studies
Master of Arts Degree, 1991 School Counseling; Emphases: Counseling and Substance Abuse

LICENSURE

National Counselor Certification
State of Michigan Counseling Certification
Private Therapist State Certification

MARTIN SYDLOSKI
Page 2

PROFESSIONAL ACTIVITIES, 1992 - Present
Conferences Attended:
Regional Crisis Intervention Consortium, Chicago, July 1994
Associative Disorder - Multiple Personalities Conference, St. Louis, May 1994
Michigan Conflict Management Conference, Detroit, November 1993
Association for Counseling and Development National Convention, New York, March 1993
State Substance Abuse Council, Battle Creek, August 1992

District Activities:
Chair, Crisis Intervention Curriculum Project, Wayne County Schools Consortium
Roundtable leader, School/Community Outreach for Youth, Detroit area agencies
Representative, Mayor's Action for Youth Council, King High School
Co-chair, Substance Abuse Prevention Council, Detroit Public Schools
Member, At-Risk Committee for Detroit Area Schools

LEADERSHIP
National Delegate, President's Council on Substance Abuse, 1994
President, Great Lakes Regional Chemical Abuse Association, 1994
Conference Chair, State Crisis Intervention Workshop, Kalamazoo, 1993
Past-president, Michigan Association for Counseling and Development, 1992
Member, Board of Directors, Youth Shelters of Detroit, 1992 - present

HONORS and AWARDS
Volunteer of the Year Award, NAACP, 1994
Outstanding Citizen Award, Detroit Chamber of Commerce, 1993
Apple Award Recipient, KRNZ Television, 1993
Blomberg Graduate Assistant Fellowship, 1991
F. J. Scotts Memorial Scholarship, 1990
Dean's List and Presidential Citation

PUBLICATIONS
"Crisis Intervention: Everyone Needs to Help," Intervention Newsletter,
Chicago, Illinois, 5(3), 1994.

"Substance Abuse and Homeless Students," Journal of Substance Abuse,
Miami, Florida, 8(2), 1992.

"Teenagers - Getting Your Attention the Hard Way," Counselor Education and Supervision,
2(3), Alexandria, Virginia, Spring, 1992.

CREDENTIALS
Education Placement Office, Any City, State 12345
Telephone: (101) 555-0008 FAX: (101) 555-0089

KENT LEHTINEN

221 College Street
Any City, State 12345
(101) 555-0009

OBJECTIVE	**Elementary School Librarian**

DEGREES

University of Wisconsin - Madison, Madison, Wisconsin
Master of Arts in Library Science, May, 1995

Bachelor of Science, August, 1990
Elementary Education, Emphasis in Reading

LIBRARY EXPERIENCE

Practicum, Central Middle School, Beloit, Wisconsin, November - December, 1994
Responsibilities:
Presented mini-lessons on using library resources to seventh-grade classes
Designed "treasure hunt" skill packets for instruction about library resources
Assisted with selection of print materials
Weeded fiction collection
Planned and developed topical exhibit for the learning resource center
Contributed and assisted with presentation of inservice program for faculty

TEACHING EXPERIENCE

Classroom Teacher, Grades 3 and 4, Unity School District, Milltown, Wisconsin, 1991-1994
Responsibilities:
Taught reading for grades 3 and 4 using whole language concepts
  to develop reading and writing skills
Utilized a variety of techniques for instruction in math and science,
  with manipulatives and hands-on approaches
Introduced computer skills in the classroom
Co-sponsored summer reading project for all third graders
Committee Assignments:
Writing Process for Elementary Grades
Elementary Computer Committee to implement computer applications
  across the curriculum for grades K-6
Outdoor Education Committee
Committee to interview superintendent candidates

ACTIVITIES & INTERESTS

Volunteer, Polk County Library System, 1992-1994
Docent, Wisconsin State Historical Society, 1995-present
Folktales and Storytelling
Genealogical Research

MEMBERSHIPS

American Library Association
American Association of School Librarians
Wisconsin Library Association
Wisconsin Education Association

CREDENTIALS

Educational Placement Office
Any City, State 12345-1338   Phone: (101) 555-0008

ANNE RYKER

221 College Street, Any City, State 12345
(101) 555-0009

OBJECTIVE

Coordinator of Media Services

EDUCATION

M.L.S. Degree - May, 1993, University of Vermont, Burlington, Vermont
Instructional Communications Technology
Area of Specialization: School Media Centers

B.A. Degree - June, 1984, Middlebury College, Middlebury, Vermont
Social Studies Education

AREAS OF EXPERTISE

Computer assisted instruction
Computer use in learning resource centers
Evaluation of instructional software
Curriculum development
Inservice programs for K-12 staff development
Program assessment of instructional materials and software

MEDIA EXPERIENCE

Media Specialist, grades 5 - 8, Hartford Middle School, White River Junction, Vermont, 1993 - present
Responsibilities:
- Establish and maintain learning centers for computer assisted instruction
- Consult with teachers planning assignments involving media and computer resources
- Evaluate, select, requisition new print or nonprint materials and computer software
- Catalog print, nonprint, and computer software materials
- Assist teachers in selecting instructional materials
- Train and supervise clerical support personnel and media center aides

TEACHING EXPERIENCE

Classroom Teacher, Longfellow Elementary School, Rosbury, Vermont, 1984-1991
Responsibilities:
- Team teacher for social studies, language arts, and science for grades three and four
- Taught individualized math and two reading groups
- Developed and maintained listening and writing centers
- Introduced computers into the classroom and taught students to use available software

RELATED ACTIVITIES

Planning Committee, Vermont Education Association
Conference on Technology and Instruction
Member, Library and Information Technology Association
Newsletter Editor, Phi Delta Kappa chapter

CREDENTIALS

Career Development Center, Any City, State 12345
(101) 555-0008 FAX: (101) 555-0089

ANTHONY LA BORDE

221 College Street
Any City, State 12345
(101) 555-0009

ACADEMIC BACKGROUND

Master of Physical Therapy 1992-1994
University of Nebraska Medical Center
Omaha, Nebraska
Bachelor of Science Degree 1988-1992
Biology
Augustana College
Sioux Falls, South Dakota

HONORS

Graduated with High Honors
Dean's List, Augustana College
Presidential Scholarship, four years

CLINICAL INTERNSHIPS

K-12 Physical Therapy, Omaha Public Schools
Omaha, Nebraska, fall 1994

Internship duties included diagnostics, consultation, direct therapy services, participation in child study committee meetings and regular conferencing with special education teachers and parents.

Neurology, University of Nebraska Physical Therapy Department
Omaha, Nebraska. May - July 1994.

Orthopedics and Acute-General, Sioux Falls Children's Hospital
Sioux Falls, South Dakota. July - August 1994.

Acute-General, Eastern Nebraska Medical Center
Lincoln, Nebraska. September - October 1994.

Internship responsibilities include evaluation and treatment of patients with varied diagnoses, discharge planning, documentation, consultation, supervision of supportive personnel, and participation in inservice programs.

ADDITIONAL CLINICAL EXPERIENCES
1992 - 1994

Participated in clinicals at facilities in Omaha, Lincoln and Sioux Falls area.

- Orthopedics
- Cardiopulmonary
- Pediatrics
- Burns

- Neurology Rehabilitation
- Acute-General
- Sports Medicine
- Nursing Home

RELATED EXPERIENCE

Physical Therapy Aide, Omaha Musculoskeletal Center, Omaha, Nebraska.
Summers and part-time, 1992 to present.

Instructed patients in exercise program and correct gait pattern preoperatively; supervised patients exercise program; treated patients using modalities.

Physical Therapy Volunteer, Veteran's Administration Hospital, Sioux Falls, 1990-1992.

Observed and assisted in physical therapy treatment. Assisted senior therapist with geriatric patients.

Counselor, Camp Sunnyside, Des Moines, Iowa. Summers, 1989-1991.

Camp counselor for handicapped children ages 5 - 18.

AFFILIATION

American Physical Therapy Association - Student Member

References Available Upon Request

ALTHEA CROSLEY

221 College Street
Any City, State 12345
(101) 555-0009

OBJECTIVE

School Nurse with responsibilities for Grades K-12

EDUCATIONAL BACKGROUND

Bachelor of Science in Nursing, Alcorn State University, Loman, Mississippi, 1995

Associate's Degree in Nursing, Coahoma Community College, Clarksdale, Mississippi, 1984

SELECTED ACADEMIC COURSES

Human Development & Behavior
Nursing Practice in Health Promotion
Health & Cultural Diversity
Psychological & Biological Aspects of Adolescence

Human Sexuality
Alcohol & Other Drug Abuse
Self-Help Groups

RECENT PROFESSIONAL DEVELOPMENT WORKSHOPS

Red Cross CPR Trainer Certification
Introduction to American Sign Language
Mandatory Reporting of Child Abuse

Treatment of Eating Disorders
Personal Health Care
Nutrition & Adult-onset Diabetes

EMPLOYMENT EXPERIENCE

Clinic Nurse (part-time), Edgewood Family Practice Clinic, Loman, Mississippi, 1993 to present
Assist physicians with physical assessments and patient care, manage patient charts and records, assist in selection, ordering, and organization of supplies.

Staff Nurse, Mercy Medical Center, Montgomery, Alabama
Pediatric Intensive Care, 1989-1993
Pediatrics, 1986-1989
Obstetrics & Gynecology, 1984-1986

REFERENCES

Available from Teacher Career Center
Any City, State 12345 Telephone: (101) 555-0008

MARK ELLSWORTH

221 College Street   Any City, State 12345   (101) 555-0009

EDUCATIONAL BACKGROUND:

Ed.S. **School Psychology**, 1995
Delta State University, Cleveland, Mississippi

M.A. **Educational Psychology**, 1990
University of Mississippi, University, Mississippi

B.A. **Elementary Education**, 1976
Livingston University, Livingston, Alabama

INTERNSHIP:

Washington County School District, Greenville, Mississippi, 1994-1995
- Administer and interpret tests of intelligence, achievement, aptitude and methods of behavioral and curriculum-based assessment.
- Write goals and objectives to meet individual needs of students, including areas of substance abuse, social skills training, therapeutic intervention, and parenting.
- Work with teachers to establish appropriate individual education plans.
- Advise parents, teachers, and students concerning educational needs and coordinate services between the family, school and other agencies.

PROFESSIONAL EXPERIENCE:

Classroom teacher, Manning Elementary, Greenville, Mississippi, 1977-1994
- Teaching experience includes: Grades 5-6   (6 years)
       Grade 2   (6 years)
       Grade 3   (5 years)
- Taught all elementary subjects except music and art.
- Expanded multicultural curriculum, introduced whole language approach to language arts and reading.
- Developed learning centers for science and mathematics which were adopted throughout the district.
- Served on district curriculum and textbook selection committees, and chaired teacher's association committees on welfare and negotiations.
- Wrote grant to acquire first classroom computer (1981).
- Coaching responsibilities included assisting with basketball and track at Solomon Junior High School and with track and golf at Weston High School

ACTIVITIES:

Coach, Babe Ruth Baseball League, 1978-1993
Volunteer coordinator, Baseball Fundraisers
Referee, Western Mississippi High School Football League
Greenville YMCA, executive committee officer for six years
Greenville Area Sunrise Rotary Club, current Past President

CREDENTIALS:

Career Planning & Placement Office
Any City, State 12345
Telephone: (101) 555-0008   FAX: (101) 555-0089

Mae Doyle

221 College Street, Any City, State 12345, (101) 555-0009 (home)
(101) 555-1111 (business)

OBJECTIVE:
School Social Worker, K-12

CURRENT PROFESSIONAL EXPERIENCE:
Family Caseworker, Bureau of Children's Services, Madison, Wisconsin, present. Responsible for coordinating home visits of all clients in central Wisconsin; arranging for medical services and follow-up on financial assistance. Promoted in 1993.

SOCIAL WORK FIELD EXPERIENCES:
School Social Worker, Milwaukee Public Schools, fall semester 1992.
Community Liaison, AIDS Coalition, West Chicago, spring semester 1992.
Caseworker, Lutheran Social Services, Chicago, summer 1991.

Additional three week internships were completed in hospice, pediatric AIDS hospital unit, and community mental health.

GRADUATE COURSE CONCENTRATIONS:

Therapy with Children	Cross-Cultural Social Work
Family Dynamics	Working with Groups
Developmentally Disabled	Racism and Discrimination

ACADEMIC TRAINING:

Master of School Social Work	Loyola University of Chicago 1991-1993 Chicago, Illinois
Bachelor of Science-Nursing	University of Evansville 1987-1991 Evansville, Indiana

PROFESSIONAL ASSOCIATIONS:
Academy of Certified Social Workers
National Association of Social Workers
American Public Health Association
Wisconsin Public Health Association

PRESENTATIONS:
"Social Workers as Children's Advocates," major address at the Great Lakes Association of Social Workers, Gary, Indiana, October, 1994.
"Teachers and Social Workers—How to Collaborate," Panel facilitator, Educators' Conference for Support Services, Chicago, Illinois, summer, 1993.
"Organizing Community Volunteers," Workshop leader, Conference on Volunteers, Wisconsin United Way Association, Green Bay, Wisconsin, spring, 1993.

REFERENCES:
Furnished Upon Request

ALLEN DE GROOT

221 College Street
Any City, State 12345
(101) 555-0009

ACADEMIC BACKGROUND

The University of Iowa	Master of Arts Degree	Speech Pathology
Iowa City, Iowa	December, 1994	
Grinnell College	Bachelor of Science	Biology
Grinnell, Iowa	August, 1992	

Will be qualified to provide speech and language services in hospitals, clinical settings and public schools, grades K-12.

PUBLIC SCHOOL EXPERIENCE

Speech Aide	Wilton Elementary School Wilton, Iowa	Fall	1992
Preschool Hearing & Language Screening	Wendell Johnson Clinic The University of Iowa	Spring	1994
Elementary Practicum	Penn Elementary School North Liberty, Iowa	Fall	1994

Worked primarily with language-impaired and learning disabled children as well as with children with language disorders.

CLINICAL EXPERIENCE

Clinic:

Wendell Johnson Speech	Articulation Disorders	Spring	1993
and Hearing Clinic	Voice Disorders	Fall	1993
The University of Iowa	Cleft Palate	Summer	1994
	Aural Rehabilitation	Fall	1994

Hospitals:

St. Luke's Methodist Hospital Cedar Rapids, Iowa	Spring	1993

Involved remediation of adults with neuropathologies of speech and language and children with language disorders.

Department of Child Psychiatry Psychiatric Hospital The University of Iowa	Spring	1993

Involved language remediation with emotionally disturbed children.

SPEECH PATHOLOGIST

TRAINING ASSIGNMENTS

Research Assistant	Otolaryngology Department University of Iowa Hospital	Fall	1993
Teaching Assistant	Clinical Procedures Course	Summer	1994

WORK EXPERIENCE

Lab Assistant	Biology Department Grinnell College	1990-1992
Counselor	Camp Sunnyside Des Moines, Iowa	Summers 1990 & 1991

COLLEGE DISTINCTIONS AND ACTIVITIES

Phi Kappa Phi
Phi Beta Kappa
Dean's List
Easter Seals Society Scholarship
National Science Foundation Undergraduate Research Grant
National Student Speech and Hearing Association

COMMUNITY SERVICE

United Way Fundraising Co-Chair	University Component Iowa City, Iowa	1994
Citizens for Environmental Action, member Iowa City, Iowa	Eastern Iowa Chapter	1992-present
Crisis Center Volunteer	Iowa City, Iowa	1992-1993

REFERENCES

Dr. Sue Pervisor	Dr. Abel Mentor	Dr. E. Val Waite
Wendell Johnson Clinic	Wendell Johnson Clinic	Wilton Community School District
The University of Iowa	The University of Iowa	Wilton, Iowa 55278
Iowa City, Iowa 52242	Iowa City, Iowa 52242	(101) 555-0102
(101) 555-0100	(101) 555-0101	

15

ADMINISTRATORS AND SUPERVISORS

KARL SCHMIDT
221 College Street
Any City, State 12345
(101) 555-0009

ADMINISTRATIVE EXPERIENCE

Coordinator of Curricular Change and Staff Development Project, Agency VI, Wheeling, West Virginia, 1994 - present
> Work directly with twelve county school districts serving more than 55,000 students in Region VI and with the University of West Virginia to develop strategies for improved instruction in secondary school mathematics and science, incorporating Scope, Sequence and Coordination program of the National Science Foundation and consistent with guidelines of the National Council of Teachers of Mathematics. Develop or coordinate informational and instructional opportunities for teachers in each district through on-site workshops, inservice, and telecommunication. Evaluate and assess program components and prepare reports for the funding agency, National Science Foundation-Systemic Initiative.

Supervisor of Student Teachers, West Virginia University, Morgantown, West Virginia, 1991-1993. Responsible for supervision and evaluation of student teachers in physical sciences; liaison with cooperating teachers in six school districts.

TEACHING EXPERIENCE

Teacher, Woodrow Wilson High School, Beckley, West Virginia, 1984-1990
Taught physics, chemistry, advanced placement chemistry; Department Chair (4 years).

Teacher, Moorefield High School, Moorefield, West Virginia, 1979-1982
> Taught physical science, physics, and chemistry.

EDUCATION

Ed.D., 1993	Curriculum and Instruction (Science Education) West Virginia University, Morgantown, West Virginia Dissertation: Evaluating the Effectiveness of Science-Technology-Society Training Programs for Middle School Science Teachers
M.S., 1983	Chemistry University of Charleston, Charleston, West Virginia
B.S., 1979	Chemistry, Minor in Mathematics Frostburg State College, Frostburg, Maryland

RECENT PRESENTATIONS

<u>Planning appropriate biology education in secondary schools.</u> Paper presented at the West Virginia Science Teachers Association Fall Conference, Charleston, West Virginia, October, 1994.

<u>Problem solving in the physical sciences.</u> Workshop for science teachers in Regional Education Service Agency VI, Wheeling, West Virginia, August, 1994.

<u>Scope, sequence, and coordination for secondary science projects.</u> Workshop for science teachers from eleven districts in Regional Educational Service Agency IV, Summersville, West Virginia, April, 1994.

<u>Environmental science materials.</u> Paper presented at Maryland Science Teachers Association Spring Conference, Frostburg, April, 1994.

<u>Teacher responses to student questions in problem solving.</u> Paper presented at the West Virginia Science Teachers Association Fall Conference, Charleston, West Virginia, October, 1993.

PROFESSIONAL MEMBERSHIPS

Association for Supervision and Curriculum Development
West Virginia Association for Supervision and Curriculum Development
National Science Supervisors Association
National Science Teachers Association
West Virginia Science Teachers Association
West Virginia Education Association

PLACEMENT FILE

Career Planning and Placement
Any City, State 12345
Telephone: (101) 555-0008
FAX: (101) 555-0089

WARREN COLSON

221 College Street
Any City, State 12345
(101) 555-0009

PROFESSIONAL OVERVIEW
Athletic Director, 3 years
Head Coach, 7 years
Teacher and Assistant Coach, 5 years

EXPERIENCE
City High School, Santa Fe Public Schools, Santa Fe, New Mexico, 1992 - present
Athletic Director and Physical Education Supervisor

Responsibilities include:
- Supervision of a comprehensive physical education curriculum and sports program for all male and female students
- Evaluation and supervision of the physical education and coaching staff
- Organize and schedule interscholastic athletic events
- Prepare and administer the department budget, order and maintain equipment
- Recruit, interview, screen, and recommend for hire potential coaches
- Conduct orientation and inservice education workshops
- Supervise athletic contests and attend appropriate professional meetings

Senior High School, Farmington Public Schools, Farmington, New Mexico, 1987 - 1991
Head Football Coach

Cibola High School, Yuma Unified High School District, Yuma, Arizona, 1984 - 1987
Head Football Coach and Head Track Coach

Mountain View Academy, Raton, New Mexico, 1979 - 1984
Business Education Teacher, Physical Education, and Assistant Coach

COACHING HIGHLIGHTS
Named Outstanding Coach of the Year, 1991
Conference Champions, 1986, 1987, and 1991
State Play-off Championship game, second place, 1987
Four players named to All-State teams

PROFESSIONAL AFFILIATIONS
National Association for Sport and Physical Education
New Mexico State Association for Football
State Association for Athletic Administrators
National Education Association

EDUCATIONAL BACKGROUND
New Mexico State University, Las Cruces, New Mexico
B.S. Degree, 1979 Major: Physical Education; Minor: Business Education
M.S. Degree, 1991 Major: Athletic Administration; Emphasis: Management

CREDENTIALS
Placement and Career Services, Any City, State 12345
Telephone: (101) 555-0008 FAX: (101) 555-0089

LUISA SERRANO

221 College Street, Any City, State 12345   (101) 555-0009

PRESENT POSITION: Business Manager, 1992-present
   East Haven Public Schools, East Haven, Connecticut
   Responsible for budget development and long-range financial planning for district
   with nearly 3,500 students and annual budget exceeding $36,000,000; establish
   and supervise uniform accounting procedures for all financial transactions;
   supervise business affairs of all supporting services; prepare monthly and annual
   reports for the Board of Education; administer group medical insurance program;
   administer all construction or maintenance contracts; develop statistical
   information for bond issues; account for all bills payable and present them to the
   Board for approval; participate in long-range facilities planning including site
   acquisition, new construction, renovation, and building maintenance.

ADDITIONAL EXPERIENCE:

   Research Assistant, 1990-1992
   College of Education, University of Connecticut, Storrs, Connecticut
   Assist with programming, scheduling, local arrangements, publicity and marketing
   for the Connecticut School Administrators Institute.

   Accountant, 1987-1990
   Hammond, Hammond & Osborne, Boston, Massachusetts

   Business Education Teacher, 1979-1987
   Ludlow Senior High School, Ludlow, Massachusetts

EDUCATION:

   Master of Arts - Educational Administration and
   Master of Business Administration, 1992
   University of Connecticut, Storrs, Connecticut

   Bachelor of Business Administration, 1986
   Boston University, Boston, Massachusetts

   Bachelor of Education - Business Education, 1979
   Bridgewater State College, Bridgewater, Massachusetts

_____ REFERENCES AVAILABLE UPON REQUEST _____

EILEEN SUTTER-HILL

221 College Street   Any City, State 12345   (101) 555-0009

PROFESSIONAL OBJECTIVE
Coordinator of Early Childhood Family Education Program

SPECIAL TRAINING

- Child development
- Family systems
- Learning environments
- Child learning styles
- Parenting issues
- Cognitive development
- Communications skills
- Early childhood curricula

EDUCATION

Graduate studies in Education and Psychology, 1994 - present
Towson State University, Baltimore, Maryland

Bachelor of Science Degree, Major: Psychology, August 1992
Coppin State College, Baltimore, Maryland

Associate Arts Degree, Area of Specialization: Education, 1988-1990
New Community College of Baltimore, Baltimore, Maryland
- Dean's List

TEACHING EXPERIENCE

Early Childhood Educator: Wood Alternative High School, Baltimore, Maryland
1992-present
> Responsible for planning and implementing the early childhood education program for parents and children birth-5 years old. Develop and obtain age-appropriate materials for use in the Early Childhood Center. Assist in long-range planning for the total program and participate in outreach and public relations activities. Conduct on-going parenting sessions for high school parents. Responsibilities also include evaluating the instructional program, which addresses the intellectual, emotional, cultural, social and physical needs of parents and children in the family education program.

Headstart Preschool Teacher: Willowwind Community Center, Baltimore, Maryland
1988-1990
> Taught a wide variety of students ages 3 years to kindergarten. Created and fostered a warm and safe learning environment. Worked closely with parents and encouraged their involvement in all activities.

CIVIC ACTIVITIES
<u>Fundraiser</u>, Free Medical Clinic, Baltimore, Maryland, 1994-present
<u>Co-director</u>, Crisis Center Food Drive, Baltimore, Maryland 1994-present
<u>Board Member</u>, Baltimore Center for Children with AIDS, 1994-present
<u>Volunteer</u>, Ecumenical Clothing Relief Project, 1994-present

PROFESSIONAL ORGANIZATIONS
National Association for the Education of Young Children
National Coalition Against AIDS
Maryland Association for Alternative Schools

Credentials available at the Career Center
Any City, State 12345 Telephone: (101) 555-0008

ALBERT NGUYEN
221 College Street
Any City, State 12345
(101) 555-0009 (home)
(101) 545-0005 (school)

PROFESSIONAL TEACHING EXPERIENCE: 14 years

San Diego Unified School District, San Diego, 1990-present
Department Chair, Social Studies Department, Henry High School

Santa Clara Unified School District, Santa Clara, 1986-1990
History teacher, Wilcox High School (grades 9-12)

Cherry Creek School District #5, Englewood, Colorado 1980-1986
Social Studies teacher, Cherry Creek High School (grades 10-12)

EXPERIENCE HIGHLIGHTS:

Participated in California Collaborative Teacher Intensive Training Program
Conducted new teacher performance evaluations and tenure review sessions
Developed collaborative teaching projects among English and history faculty
Received state educational grant for advanced placement course training
Directed the state-wide Advanced Placement European History Curriculum Project
Editor for a national newsletter for advanced placement history teachers

CURRENT COMMITTEE LEADERSHIP:

Member, California Committee for Talented and Gifted High School Students
Chair, San Diego Social Studies Curriculum Revision Project
Faculty Representative, Superintendent's Parent Advisory Board
Regional Consortium Delegate, State Department of Public Education 2000

PROFESSIONAL MEMBERSHIPS:

Association for Supervision and Curriculum Development
Society for History Education
Council for European Studies
American Historical Association

ACADEMIC BACKGROUND:

Stanford University, Stanford, California
M.A. Medieval History (1985)   Ph.D. Curriculum and Instruction (1992)
Santa Clara State University, Santa Clara, California
B.A. European History and Middle Eastern Studies (1980)

SPECIAL RECOGNITION, 1990-present:

Commencement Speaker (chosen by senior class) 1990, 1991, 1993
Governor's Award for Outstanding Work with Talented and Gifted, 1993
Appointed to President's Council on Learning, 1993
Outstanding Teacher Award, Stanford University, 1994
Selected for United Nations Middle East Study Trip, 1995

REFERENCES AVAILABLE UPON REQUEST AT
Career Planning & Placement Center
Any City, State 12345
(101) 555-0008 FAX: (101) 555-1118

EMILY SUNDBERG
221 College Street
Any City, State 12345
(101) 555-0009 (home)
(101) 555-1111 (school)

EDUCATIONAL EXPERIENCE SUMMARY

Graduate Research Assistant	The University of Iowa	1994-present
Director of Personnel	Council Bluffs, Iowa	1992-1994
Coordinator of Curriculum & Instruction	Bering Strait, Alaska	1988-1992
Language Arts/Chapter One Coordinator	Avon, Massachusetts	1985-1988
Secondary English Teacher	Agana, Guam	1980-1983

PROFESSIONAL EXPERIENCE

Director of Personnel, Council Bluffs Community School District, Council Bluffs, Iowa, 8/92 - 7/94. Planned, developed and revised personnel management regulations in accordance with Board policy. Organized effective and appropriate procedures to recruit, select, and retain quality staff. Monitored the ongoing success of the district's personnel efforts and supervised the day-to-day personnel activities. Implemented a minority recruitment process including the planning of recruitment trips, compilation of data, screening, interviewing, and maintenance of records. Developed staffing plans and recommended teaching assignments and district-wide transfers. Assisted in staff reductions, terminations, and recall proceedings.

Coordinator of Curriculum & Instruction, Bering Strait School District, Unalakleet, Alaska, 1988-1992. Worked cooperatively with staff and administrators on curriculum issues in 16 villages spanning 80,000 square miles of rugged terrain. Facilitated major revision of intermediate curriculum, replacing current programs with integrated and developmentally appropriate practices. With staff collaboration, developed a state recognized K-8 literacy program. Established a business/school partnership to create and equip innovative computer labs. Designed intensive staff development plan to support curricular change.

Language Arts/Chapter One Coordinator, Avon Public Schools, Avon, Massachusetts, 1985-1988. Responsibilities included organizing and directing K-12 services in reading and language arts. Worked with staff to implement process writing, whole language methodology, reading in the content areas, children's literature, alternative assessment, thinking skills infusion, and multiple intelligence theory. Developed action teams to include staff at all levels.

Secondary English Teacher, Washington High School, Department of Education, Agana, Guam, 1980-1983. Taught English 9, Honors 10 classes and Creative Writing, an elective class offered through after school extended learning programs. Advisor of the school newspaper, <u>The Banana Leaf</u>.

ADMINISTRATIVE STRENGTHS

- Provide leadership for the planning, coordinating, supervising, and evaluation of all personnel services including recruitment, selection, and assignment of staff.
- Knowledge of state and federal guidelines and legislation (e.g. ADA, Affirmative Action, Civil Rights Act, Age Discrimination) regarding hiring practices and selection procedures.
- Experience in and support for shared decision making and site based management principles and practices.
- Ability to collaborate and work as a team member with management and the Board of Education, professional and support staff, students, parents, and community.
- Experience with system-wide information management and data-based decision making.

GRADUATE ASSISTANTSHIPS

Research Assistant, Institute for School Executives, College of Education, The University of Iowa, 1995 - present. Assist with the planning and organization of four major institutes per year. Invite renowned speakers from across the nation to address school administrators from across the state. Participated in preparation of a grant funded by the Geraldine Dodge Foundation.

Supervisor of Student Teachers, College of Education, The University of Iowa, 1994 - 1995. Responsibilities included supervising, advising and evaluating thirteen secondary student teachers. Worked with public school teachers and administrators in a variety of settings. Presented workshops on classroom management, development of lesson plans, teaching strategies and salary negotiations.

Emily Sundberg
page 2

DEGREES

Ph.D.   **Planning, Policy & Leadership Studies**
The University of Iowa, Iowa City, Iowa, June 1996
Projected Dissertation Topic: Analysis of Prescribed
Interview Styles and Candidate Ranking

M.A.   **Mass Communication**
Johns Hopkins University, Baltimore, Maryland, May 1985
Emphasis: Institutional Public Relations

B.S.   **English and Mass Communication**
University of Guam, Mangilao, Guam, June 1980
Phi Beta Kappa
Graduated with highest distinction

MEMBERSHIPS

Member, American Association of School Personnel Administrators (AASPA)
Board Member, Alaska Association of School Personnel Administrators
Member and Advisory Committee Member, International Reading Association
Past President, Alaska Council on Reading
Member, Association for Supervision and Curriculum Development
State Treasurer ('88), Massachusetts Association for Supervision and Curriculum Development

LICENSURE

Iowa Professional Administrator's License; Superintendent (PK-12) Endorsement
Alaska and Massachusetts Administrative and Teaching Certificates; Endorsements: Supervisor of
    Personnel Services and Supervisor of Curriculum

RECENT SEMINARS & CONFERENCES

State Leadership Conference, Iowa Association for School Administrators, Des Moines, Iowa, October 1995
AASPA Symposium on Management Innovations, San Diego, California, July 1995
AASPA National Convention, Washington, D.C., October 1994
Alaska Association for Bilingual Education, Fairbanks, Alaska, May 1994
Iowa Language Arts Conference (invited speaker), Drake University, Des Moines, Iowa, May 1994
Northwest Regional States Conference on Outcome Based Education, Seattle, Washington, March 1993

SPECIAL RECOGNITION

Distinguished Teacher Award, The University of Iowa, 1995
Distinguished Young Alumni Award, Johns Hopkins University, 1992
Alaska Kiwanis Volunteer-of-the-Year Recipient, Anchorage, Alaska, 1990
Omicron Delta Kappa Upperclass Leadership Honor Society, 1980
Fulbright Undergraduate Scholar, 1979

References provided upon request.

JAMES DOLMAN _____

221 College Street, Any City, State 12345, (101) 555-0009 (home)
(101) 555-1111 (school)

OVERVIEW:

• Headmaster	10 years	• **Teacher**	5 years
• Adjunct Professor	5 years	• **International**	
• Principal	6 years	**Volunteer**	2 years

CURRENT EXPERIENCE:

Headmaster, The Antilles School, St. Thomas, Virgin Islands, 1984-present. Administrative responsibility for The Antilles School—an independent college preparatory day school offering instruction from early childhood to grade 12. Student body comprises 430 students from diverse racial, ethnic and national origins. The 27 acre campus consists of five separate classroom buildings, two libraries and numerous athletic fields.

Adjunct Professor, College of Education, University of Virgin Islands, St. Thomas 1989-present. Teaching responsibility for the on-site methods component of the Social Science Methods class. Students are introduced to lesson design, classroom management strategies, teaching styles, test construction, and evaluation methods.

PROFESSIONAL EXPERIENCES:

Principal, St. Margaret's School, San Juan Capistrano, California, 1981 - 1985
Principal/Lead Teacher, Libreville Day School, Libreville, Gabon, 1978 - 1980
K-12 Teacher, Libreville Boys' School, Libreville, Gabon, 1976 - 1978
Secondary Teacher, Aiken High School, Aiken, South Carolina, 1973 - 1976
Volunteer, Heifer Project International, Ghana, South America, 1971 - 1973

SPECIAL TRAINING & INSTITUTES:

Oxford University, Oxford, England, Summer 1993
    Topic: Global Learning and Social Responsibility
Teacher's College, Columbia University, New York, Summer 1991
    Topic: Management by Consensus
Princeton University, Princeton, New Jersey, Summer 1989
    Topic: New School Concept
University of Montana, Missoula, Montana, Summer 1987
    Topic: Grantwriting for Private Schools

ACADEMIC TRAINING:

Educational Specialist Degree	University of South Carolina, 1981
	Columbia, South Carolina
Bachelor of Arts Degree	Reed College, 1971
Social Science and Psychology	Portland, Oregon

PROFESSIONAL MEMBERSHIPS:

Middle States Association of Schools and Colleges
National Association of Independent Schools
Caribbean Counselors Association
National Association of Secondary School Principals
American Association for Counseling and Development

References provided upon request _____

MARIA MIGENES

221 College Street
Any City, State 12345
(101) 555-0009 (home)
(101) 555-0089 (office)
MMigenes@Georgetown.GU.edu (email)

EDUCATIONAL EXPERIENCE

Fall 1995 — **Administrative Intern**, Central Administrative Office, District of Columbia School District, Washington, D.C. Assisted in all phases of long-range demographic planning for the district. Planning team was led by the Associate Superintendentand an urban geographer from Georgetown University.

1995 — **Research Assistant**, Institute for School Administrators, Georgetown University. Researched and team planned seminar topics for administrators. Topics included technology in education, sexual harassment and school policies, Americans with Disabilities Act, bloodborne pathogens literature and school procedures.

1990-1993 — **Assistant Building Principal, grades K - 5**
Alvord United School District, Riverside, California

1992-1993 — **Spanish Instructor-Bilingual Teacher Training Program**
University of California-Riverside

1988-1990 — **Elementary Teacher, grade 4**
Mentor Teacher (ESL emphasis)
American School, San Salvador, El Salvador

1986-1988 — **Bilingual Classroom Teacher, grades 2/3**
Jurupa United School District, Riverside, California

EDUCATIONAL BACKGROUND

Master of Arts Degree in Educational Administration, December 1995
Georgetown University, Washington, D.C.

Bachelor of Arts Degree in Elementary Education - Bilingual Emphasis, May 1986
California State University, San Bernadino, California

TRAVEL & LANGUAGES

Traveled in Honduras, Guatemala, Costa Rica, El Salvador and Argentina
Rotary Foreign Exchange Student, Tegucigalpa, Honduras, Fall, 1979
Attended International School of Aruba, San Nicolas, Aruba, 1980 -1982
Language abilities in Spanish (bilingual) and French (conversationally fluent)

PROFESSIONAL ACTIVITIES

Committee participation:
- Co-chair, Graduate Student Advisory Committee, 1994 - present
- Graduate Student Representative, Five-year Program Review Committee, 1994
- Chair, English Language Development Committee, 1993
- Vice-chair, Bilingual Curriculum Committee, 1992 - 1993
- Member, Student Attendance Review Board, 1992 - 1993
- Member, Multi-cultural Curriculum Review Committee, 1991
- Member, Student Study Team, 1991
- Leadership Team Member, Program Quality Review, 1989 - 1990

Inservice presentations:
- Monolingual Teachers and Bilingual Students: How Can We Communicate?
- Cooperative Learning Projects in the Bilingual Classroom
- Understanding Cultural Differences and the ESL Student

Special projects:
- Desert Cities Regional Reading Council
- Strategic Planning Board for Alvord United School District
- Community Parent Outreach Project
- School/Business Alliance of Riverside County

Recent conferences:
- Annual Meeting of the National Association of Elementary School Principals Orlando, Florida, March 1994
- Association of Overseas Educators, Indiana, Pennsylvania, Fall 1993
- Western Regional Meeting of Bilingual Educators, Provo, Utah, Spring 1992

PROFESSIONAL AFFILIATIONS

National Association of Elementary School Principals
Association for Supervision and Curriculum Development
California Women in Educational Leadership
Association of Overseas Educators

LICENSURE

Provisional Professional Officer Certificate - District of Columbia
Professional Credential and Multiple Subjects Credential - State of California
Language Development Specialist Endorsement - State of California

SPECIAL RECOGNITION

Distinguished Teacher of the Year Award, California State University
Georgetown University Graduate Thesis Award for Outstanding Research
Graduate Leadership Award, College of Education, Georgetown University
Undergraduate Achievement Scholarship, California State University

CREDENTIALS

Educational Placement Office, Any City, State 12345   Telephone: (101) 555-0008

DONALD BOCCIO

221 College Street
Any City, State 12345
(101) 555-0009 (home)
(101) 555-0089 (office)

OBJECTIVE: **High School Principal**

EDUCATION:

Point Park College, Pittsburgh, Pennsylvania
    M.S. Degree - Educational Administration - August 1993 to May 1995
       Thesis: "Personnel Selection Factors: Criteria and Process for Screening"

Claremont Graduate School, Claremont, California
    Scholar-in-Residence Summer Program, 1994
       Topic: Educational Administration in Urban Schools

Slippery Rock University, Slippery Rock, Pennsylvania
    B.S. Degree, Physics, 1987
    summa cum laude

ADMINISTRATIVE EXPERIENCE:

High School Assistant Principal, Oliver High School, Pittsburgh, Pennsylvania,
<u>Major responsibilities 1990 - present</u>:

- Direct responsibility for the supervision of the computerized records management system including grade reporting, attendance and permanent records.
- Responsible for student disciplinary procedures for fifty percent of the student body; also included follow-up and parental conferences.
- Conducted performance evaluations of the science and math faculty members.
- Supervised day-to-day instructional budget operations.
- Worked closely with the Allegheny County Sheriff's Liaison Program.
- Involved with the Pittsburg Center for Alcohol and Drug Services.

TEACHING EXPERIENCE:

Physics Teacher, Oliver High School, Pittsburgh, Pennsylvania, 1987 - 1990
<u>Responsibilities</u>:

- Taught Physics, Science Research and AP Physics
- Sponsored the Science Club and organized the Space Fair

ACTIVITIES & AFFILIATIONS:

- Strategic Planning Action Team Member, 1993
- Negotiation Team Member for Pittsburgh Administrators' Association, 1993
- Co-chair of Discipline Review Committee, 1992
- NCA Steering Evaluation Committee Member, Oliver High School, 1992
- Pittsburgh New Schools Development Corporation Regional Member, 1991-1992
- Chair, Vocational Education Study Committee, 1991
- Co-chair, Site-based Management Committee, 1989-1990
- President, Pittsburgh Science Association, 1990
- National Association of Secondary School Principals
- School Administrators of Pennsylvania

CREDENTIALS ON FILE:

Teacher Career Center
Any City, State 12345 (101) 555-0008

BARBARA KLEIN

221 College Street
Any City, State 12345
(101) 555-0009

PROFESSIONAL OVERVIEW
- Special Education Consultant   3 years
- Education Prescriptionist   4 years
- Special Education Teacher   5 years
- Behavior Management Specialist   2 years

COMPETENCIES

Special Education Supervision	Compliance Monitoring
Inservice Training	Psycho-educational Testing
Collaborative Consultation	Diagnostic-Prescriptive Teaching

CONSULTING AND SUPERVISORY EXPERIENCE
Educational Service Unit 31, Cheney, Washington, 1993 - present
Behavior Disorder Specialist and General Special Education Consultant

Department of Defense Dependents Schools, Munich, Germany, 1989 - 1993
Educational Prescriptionist

Mississippi Bend Area Educational Agency, Bettendorf, Iowa, 1987 - 1989
Special Education Consultant

Responsibilities in the above positions included:
- Supervision of special education programs preK - 12 grades
- Consulting with parents, administrators, teachers and referral agencies
- Coordination with state and local programs in designing projects and writing grants
- Providing assistance in curricula, program, IEP development, and pre-intervention
- Assisting schools in compliance with federal and state special education regulations
- Furnishing inservice training programs to parents, schools, and outside agencies
- Giving psycho-educational testing and participating in interdisciplinary team staffings
- Training staff in techniques for dealing with behavior problem students

CLASSROOM EXPERIENCE
International School of Helsinki, Helsinki, Finland, 1985 - 1987
Behavior Disorders and Learning Disabilities Teacher
Senior Class Advisor; Sophomore Girl's Basketball Coach

Cooperative Education Service Unit, Elm Grove, Wisconsin, 1981 - 1985
Secondary Special Education Multi-disability Resource Teacher
Faculty Advisor to Students Against Drunk Driving Club

Kauai School District, Waimea, Kauai, 1979 - 1981
Behavior Specialist and In-school Suspension Teacher
Intramural Director

PROFESSIONAL AFFILIATIONS
Association for Overseas Educators
American Association for Curriculum and Development
Washington Association for Exceptional Children
National Association of Supervisors and Directors of Secondary Education

BARBARA KLEIN
page 2

EDUCATIONAL BACKGROUND
University of Hawaii-Manoa, Honolulu, Hawaii
Bachelor of Science Degree, 1974 Major: Special Education (K - 12)
Master of Arts Degree, 1985 Behavior Disorders

Additional special education graduate coursework completed at:
University of Washington, Seattle
Michigan State University - Summer Campus, Cyprus
Iowa State University, Ames

LICENSURE
Minnesota dual licensure in Emotional/Behavior Disabilities and Learning Disabilities
Iowa and Washington Supervisory (K-12) Special Education Certificates
Washington licensure in Emotional/Behavior, Learning Disabled and General
Special Education

CURRENT PROFESSIONAL ACTIVITIES
Training sessions:
"Orientation Programs and New Staff Success," staff training sessions presented at six
regional centers in Oregon and Washington, 1993 - present

"Quality Assurance/Peer Review Programs," supervisory training sessions offered for referral
agencies and special education service units in Washington, 1993 - 1994

"Understanding and Monitoring Rules and Regulations with Third Party Systems," in-house
training sessions for directors of various departments, Cheney, Washington, 1993 - 1994

Committees:
Chair, Northwest Regional Special Education Staff Consortium
Chair, Orientation Review Committee, Educational Service Unit I
Member, Computerized Special Education Resources Inventory System

TRAVEL AND INTERNATIONAL INTERESTS
- Travels in England, Germany, France, Switzerland, Italy,
  Cyprus, Jordan, Egypt, Kenya, Morocco, Spain and China
- Co-founder, ASIA Outreach Program, Cheney, Washington
- Host Family, Foreign Field Service Students
- Member, International Woman's Club
- Volunteer, Americares Association

MILITARY SERVICE
United States Air Force, Second Lieutenant - Air Borne Division, 1974 - 1978
Awarded commendations for flight training and flight performance, 3 years

CREDENTIALS
Education Placement Office, Any City, State 12345
Telephone: (101) 555-0008 FAX: (101) 555-0089

MELANIE HAYES

221 College Street	Any City, State 12345	(101) 555-0009

DEGREES

Ph.D. Educational Administration, August 1994
Syracuse University, Syracuse, New York
Dissertation: History of Pre-service Training: Success and Failure of New Teachers

Master of Arts Degree, Educational Policy, June 1988
Trenton State College, Trenton, New Jersey
   • Graduate Fellow

Master of Arts Degree, Music Education, May 1982
Queens College-City University of New York, New York

Bachelor of Music Degree, Major: Theory, August 1980
Eastman School of Music, Rochester, New York

PROFESSIONAL EXPERIENCE SUMMARY
   • **Superintendent of Schools**, Westhill Schools, Syracuse, New York, 1992 - present
   • **Assistant Superintendent for Curriculum and Instruction**, Upper Township Schools,
      Tuckahoe, New Jersey, 1990 - 1992
   • **Principal**, Upper Township Middle School, Tuckahoe, New Jersey, 1987 - 1990
   • **Assistant Principal**, Fleming Middle School, Trenton, New Jersey, 1984 - 1987
   • **Vocal Music Teacher**, PS #50 Talfourd Lawn School, Queens District #28
      Jamaica, New York, 1981 - 1984
   • **Singer**, New York City Clubs, 1980 - 1981

CIVIC ACTIVITIES
   <u>President</u>, Northside Repertory Company, 1995
   <u>Board Member</u>, Syracuse American Red Cross Chapter, 1994 - present
   <u>Co-director</u>, Chamber of Commerce Leadership Series, 1994 - present
   <u>Board Member</u>, Friends of the Syracuse Public Library, 1993 - 1994
   <u>Volunteer Director</u>, City Girls' Choir and Performing Troupe, 1992 - 1994

RECOGNITION
   Awarded Certificate of Merit, New York Music Teachers' Association
   Awarded Outstanding Doctoral Student Scholarship by Syracuse University
   Named New Jersey Middle School Principal of the Year, 1990
   Listed in *Who's Who in Education*

PROFESSIONAL ORGANIZATIONS
   National Association of Secondary Principals
   American Association of School Administrators
   Association for Supervision and Curriculum Development

CURRENT PROFESSIONAL SERVICE
   Chair, Steering Committee, Performance-based Compensation
   Chair, Committee for Education Extended Beyond the Classroom
   Board Member, School Administrators of New York
   Representative, Governor's Commission on New Schools
   President, State Women's Caucus for Administrators

Complete list of publications and presentations available upon request

NONCERTIFIED TEACHERS— PRIVATE SCHOOLS

GINA ALIOTO
221 College Street
Any City, State 12345
(101) 555-1111

ACADEMIC BACKGROUND

School for International Training, Brattleboro, Vermont   June 1994
M.A. Counseling and Human Development   Emphasis: Student Personnel

Norwich University, Northfield, Vermont   May 1990
B.A. Economics and English

Hotchkiss School, Lakeville, Connecticut   May 1986
Diploma with Honors

EXPERIENCE

Resident Advisor and Secondary Teacher, Cranbrook Schools, Bloomfield Hills, Michigan, August 1994 - present. Responsibilities include advising and counseling students with academic or personal concerns; intervening in crisis and conflict situations and coordinating the educational, recreational and social programming of a 370 member residence hall. Teaching duties include senior level Economics and sophomore Composition. Maintain close communication with faculty and administration concerning student progress in weekly staff meetings.

Hall Coordinator, Department of Residence Services, The University of Maine, 1990 - 1992. Responsible for the overall organization, administration, and supervision of a co-ed undergraduate hall of 400 students. Selected, trained, and evaluated a staff consisting of seven resident assistants and four clerical staff. Specific duties encompassed facility management, counseling, discipline and advising hall government.

Graduate Assistant- Student Affairs, Division of University Housing, School for International Training, 1992 - 1994. Assisted in the advising and supervision of eight student staff members in two separate units of 600 students. Responsible for implementation of administration policies, personal/academic concerns of residents and hall council.

Tutor, Hartford Public Schools Summer Reading Program, Hartford, Connecticut, 1988 and 1989. Worked with individual students to maintain their current reading level or to develop new strategies in learning to read. Worked with middle school age students in an inner city setting.

ACTIVITIES & AFFILIATIONS

Participant, International Round Table, University/Community Consortium,
      Detroit, Michigan, 1994 - present
International Partner Program, Office of International Affairs, Brattleboro, Vermont, 1993
Teacher, International Preschool & Tutoring Center, Brattleboro, Vermont, 1993
Resident Assistant, Norwich University, Northfield, Vermont, 1988 - 1990
Lived in Jordan and Saudi Arabia - attended international schools from 1980 - 1984
Active membership in Michigan Student Personnel Association, American College Personnel
      Association, and American Association for Counseling & Development

References provided upon request.

DEAN HUGHES
221 College Street
Any City, State 12345
(101) 555-0009

TEACHING COMPETENCIES

Painting	Printmaking	Ceramics
Drawing	Design	Sculpture

TEACHING EXPERIENCE

Teacher Incentive Program (TIP), Kentucky Arts Council, 1994-1995
> In collaboration with teachers in Kentucky schools, developed projects to enhance visual arts instruction. Designed and implemented innovative projects including thirteen residencies ranging from one to three weeks, with emphasis on printmaking, painting, and collage. As artist-in-residence, worked directly with students of all ages, kindergarten through high school.

Art Instructor, Louisville Art Guild, Louisville, Kentucky, 1994
> Taught weekly evening classes for adults in drawing, painting (oils, acrylics, watercolor), and woodcuts. Saturday morning classes for children included instruction in drawing and ceramics.

Teaching Assistant, University of Kentucky, Louisville, Kentucky, 1992-1994
> Responsible for instruction and supervision of lithography studio for undergraduate art majors.

EXHIBITIONS

Juried Shows:
> Purchase Prize, 46th Annual Artists Showcase, Louisville Public Library, 1994
> Invitational, Wimsee Art Center, Knoxville, Kentucky, 1994
> Honorable Mention, Louisville Annual Art in the Park Celebration, 1993

Solo Exhibits:
> Louisville Art Association, 1994
> University of Kentucky DeWare Gallery, 1994
> Avenue C Gallery, Louisville, Kentucky, 1993

EDUCATION

M.F.A. 1994   Printmaking, University of Kentucky, Louisville, Kentucky

B.A.   1991   Art and Art History, Winthrop College, Rock Hill, South Carolina

REFERENCES

Emma Sue Pervisor	Annie Person	Art DeLer
Kentucky Arts Council	Louisville Art Guild	Avenue C Gallery
(101) 555-0101	(101) 555-0102	(101) 555-0100

JUNE ENGLUND
221 College Street
Any City, State 12345
(101) 555-1111

OBJECTIVE
Professional position in a multicultural environment.

SPECIAL SKILLS
- Able to work with people of diverse backgrounds and skill levels.
- Skilled in program development, behavior strategies and staff management.
- Open-minded, flexible, patient and a cooperative team member.
- Speak Spanish; knowledgeable about cultural differences.

EDUCATION
Graduate Studies in Psychology, Rollins College, Winter Park, Florida, 1992 - present
B.A. Psychology and Religion, Palm Beach Atlantic College, West Palm Beach, Florida, 1989

TEACHING EXPERIENCE
Kindergarten Teacher, South Miami Lutheran School, Miami, Florida, 1993 - present.
- Plan, instruct, and evaluate kindergartners' cognitive, social, gross and fine motor development using self-prepared lesson plans.
- Prepare lessons that emphasized cooperative and multicultural learning.
- Use creativity and variety to interest students in classroom activities.
- Maintain frequent parental contact through conferences, telephone conversations and weekly newsletters.

Migrant Head Start Supervisor, Broward County Migrant Child and Family Services, Davie, Florida, 1991 -1993.
- Organized the child care needs, health and education of prreschool children of migrant agricultural workers.
- Worked with teachers in full-day and extended day programs in nine different centers.
- Collaborated with health professionals who addressed the daily and on-going health needs of the children.

Assistant Director and Preschool Teacher, Mercy Child Development Center, Pensacola, Florida, 1989 - 1991.
- Developed and implemented summer school enrichment program.
- Supervised staff, trained new teachers, conducted staff meetings, and developed budget.
- Taught four year olds in pre-kindergarten classroom.

VOLUNTEER ACTIVITIES
Volunteer reader, Hear Me Read Program, Miami Public Library
Program Chair, Teenage Parents' Retreat, YWCA, West Palm Beach
Friends Youth Program, Longmont State Mental Hospital, Pensacola

PROFESSIONAL SERVICE
Board Member, Florida Migrant Education Council, Tallahassee, 1994 - present
Presenter, Child Care Conference of Southern Florida, Miami, October, 1994
Conference Chair, Florida Conference on Migrant Education, Ft. Lauderdale, Fall, 1993
Key address, Governor's Conference on Migrant Education, Tallahassee, Spring, 1993
Co-author, *Child Care on the Move*, staff manual prepared for Migrant Family Services, 1993

References provided upon request.

LINDA HASLER

221 College Street
Any City, State 12345
(101) 555-0009

OBJECTIVE: **French or German teacher in a private setting.**
Extracurricular interests in crew and language clubs.

EDUCATION: Teacher Training Course, The Shady Hill School
Cambridge, Massachusetts, 1994-1995
(Post-graduate year of apprenticeship in teaching)

Yale University, New Haven, Connecticut
Bachelor of Arts Degree - May 1994
    Majors: French and German
    with distinction and honor

Institute of European Studies, Nantes, France
Program in French language and culture, 1993

TEACHING
APPRENTICE: **Apprentice Language Teacher**, The Shady Hill School
    Cambridge Massachusetts, School year, 1994 - 1995

Responsibilities:
* Taught French classes, levels I, II and III, and beginning German
  under the tutelage of the Directing Teacher
* Used various teaching techniques to allow for differing learning styles
* Provided tutorial services for students needing additional help
* Evaluated student progress and held regular student conferences
* Monitored language lab and assisted students with computer software
* Observed and participated in numerous workshops, seminars, and conferences
  throughout the year
* Organized, in conjunction with the History Department, a Cultural Fair
  highlighting language, customs and historical perspectives

RELATED
EXPERIENCES: **Senior Counselor**, Concordia Language Villages, Moorhead, Minnesota
Summer 1994
Responsibilities:
* Taught French language skills to villagers of all ages
* Organized and led large and small group activities
* Maintained a high energy level while dealing with repetition
* Related to villagers on a personal level as a teacher and a counselor

YWCA Counselor, Minnetonka Day Camp, Minnetonka, Minnesota
Summer 1993
Responsibilities:
* Taught nature lore and environmental awareness units
* Coordinated day-long canoe trips for campers in all age groups

149

School Bus Driver, Cambridge Coach Company, New Haven, Connecticut
Summer school sessions and part-time, 1992 - 1993
Responsibilities:
- Interacted effectively with students, parents, and school staff
- Maintained discipline under adverse conditions

ACTIVITIES:
- Coxswain, Yale Crew Team, 3 years
- Elected Captain of the Yale Crew Team, 1994
- Advanced to crew national competition (6th place)
- Member, New Haven Chapter, United Nations Organization
- Volunteer, Host Family Volunteers - International Student Association
- Treasurer, International Dormitory

AWARDS:
Recontres Internationales de Jeunes a Avignon (achievement scholarship) 1993
Honors House Member, 1992 - 1994
National Merit Scholar, 1991

TRAVEL:
France, Germany, England, Netherlands and Greece
Lived with a French family in 1993. Traveled and visited museums, cathedrals, and historical sites in all countries.

LANGUAGES:
Excellent command of French and German (near native fluency)
Moderate abilities in Spanish and Greek

INTERESTS:
Sailing, philately, and wilderness expeditions

CREDENTIALS ON FILE:
Career Planning and Placement Center
Any City, State 12345 (101) 555-0008

GREGORY TAKIS

409 University Avenue
Any City, State 12345
Phone; (101) 555-0009
EMAIL: TAKIS@HUBACS.BITNET

OBJECTIVE:
Classroom teacher:	History
Extracurricular:	Sponsor for Academic Decathlon, Knowledge Bowl, and Model United Nations; Rugby Coach

EDUCATION:

Hofstra University, Hempstead, New York
   Ph.D. European History - May 1995
   Comprehensive Areas: Medieval Europe, Europe (1500-1815)
      and Women in Early Societies

Kings College, Cambridge University, Cambridge, England
   Medieval Studies - 1992

State University of New York at Albany, Albany, New York
   M.A. Renaissance History - 1990   B.A. History and Art - 1988

The Haverford School, Haverford, Pennsylvania
   Diploma with honors - 1985

RELATED EXPERIENCE:

Teaching Assistant, History Department, Hofstra University, 1994 - present
Responsibilities include the instruction and grading of a two-semester course entitled Economic and Social History of Medieval Europe. Organized extra study and review sessions and maintained regular office hours for student appointments.

Academic Tutor, Athletic Department, Hofstra University, 1993
Responsibilities included working individually with athletes who needed assistance with research papers and test preparation.

PEACE CORPS:

Community Development, Arish, Yemen, 1990 and 1991
Worked with several village leaders to develop water delivery systems and to improve drinking water quality.

ACTIVITIES & AWARDS:

- United Nations Graduate Intern Fellowship, Summer, 1994
- Representative, Graduate Student Senate, 1992
- Member, American Historical Association
- Member, Renaissance Society of America
- John T. McMellon History Award, 1991
- President, International Club, 1990
- Presidential Scholar, 1985-1988

CREDENTIALS ON FILE:

University Placement Service
Any City, State 12345 (101) 555-0008

MATTHEW HORTON

PRESENT ADDRESS
221 College St.
Any City, State 12345
(101) 555-0009

PERMANENT ADDRESS
12 Royal Avenue
Mytown, State 23456
(909) 333-0003

TEACHING INTERESTS
Orchestra Director and Strings Teacher

ACADEMIC TRAINING
The University of Akron, Akron, Ohio
Master of Arts Degree, Conducting, August, 1995

Oberlin College, Oberlin, Ohio
Bachelor of Music Degree, May, 1992
Major: Music Appreciation   Specialization: Strings

INTERNSHIP
***Strings - elementary and secondary level**, St. Mary's Private Academy
Cleveland, Ohio, Spring, 1995*

Responsibilities of the internship included:
- Taught individualized lessons to strings players, grades 4 through 6
- Instructed elementary string students using the Suzuki method
- Arranged recitals for students to gain exposure and recognition
- Created a positive environment for students of all abilities
- Rehearsed 80-piece orchestra for major spring concert
- Conducted orchestra during All-State rehearsal
- Evaluated student progress and maintained contact with parents and private strings instructors

VOLUNTEER EXPERIENCE
Orchestra, grades 9 - 12, Washington High School, Oberlin, Ohio, Fall, 1994
- Worked extensively with violin and viola players
- Introduced new music to the advanced orchestra
- Assisted with the conducting of the Concert Strings Symphony

MUSIC ACTIVITIES & DISTINCTIONS
Featured Soloist, Winter Symphony Festival, Cleveland, 1995
Orchestra member, Cleveland City Orchestra, 1994 - present
First Chair, Violin, The University of Akron Symphony, 1994
First Chair, Violin, Oberlin Symphony, 1991 - 1993

HONORS
Conductor's Medal, The University of Akron, 1995
Graduate Fellowship in Music, The University of Akron, 1994
Oberlin Music Medallion for Outstanding Achievement, 1992
Dean's Academic Scholarship,Oberlin College, 1990 - 1992

References Provided Upon Request

BRIAN MAX

221 College Street
Any City, State 12345
(101) 555-0009

PROFESSIONAL EXPERIENCE

Abington Friends School, Jenkintown, Pennsylvania, 1990 - present
<u>Skills Lab Instructor, grades 9-12</u>
Work with individual students in all academic areas. Determine needs of students and supplement with appropriate learning materials. Coordinate with teachers the best approach for students' academic success. Expanded skills lab to include computer-aided instruction, electronic bulletin boards and written materials appropriate for all skill levels.

<u>Team Leader</u>, Mexico Workcamp, May - July, 1994
Chaperoned 15 students on a workcamp trip to central Mexico. Lived in a rural area with local families and assisted in field work, village building projects, road maintenance and child care.

INTERNSHIP

Friends Academy, North Dartmouth, Massachusetts, August 1989 - May 1990
<u>Food Service Intern</u>
Assisted Food Coordinator in planning and producing nourishing and appealing meals for students and staff. Food choices involved meat, vegetarian dishes and vegan dishes. Worked mostly in evenings and week-ends. Supervised and instructed students interested or assigned to food preparation. Intern responsibilities also included living in the dormitory and assuming daily duties.

RELATED ACTIVITIES

- Traveled with students on work trips to Belize, Jamaica, Haiti and Mexico
- Studied "Landfill Archaeology" at the University of Arizona, Summer 1993
- Attended Yale Summer Institute on the Rebirth of Classics for Secondary Students
- Facilitator for panel discussion on *Academic Success of Boarding School Students from Foreign Countries* at Independent Educational Services Conference, San Francisco

WORK EXPERIENCE

Night-shift Chef, Hamburg Inn, Canton, Ohio, June 1990 - December 1990
Assistant Night Manager, McDonalds, Canton, Ohio, 1987 - 1989
Line Server, Dettermine Dormitory, Malone College, 1986 - 1987

EDUCATIONAL BACKGROUND

Malone College, Canton, Ohio
    Bachelor of Arts Degree, 1985 - 1990
    Majors: Archaeology, Philosophy and Latin

Friends Academy, Locust Valley, New York
    High School Diploma, 1985
    Friends' Scholar Distinction
    National Merit Scholar

REFERENCES

Dr. Ed Master, Abington Friends School, (101) 555-0101
Mr. Abel Mentor, Dean of Students, Malone College, (101) 555-0102

ELIZABETH DAVIS
221 College Street
Any City, State 12345
(101) 555-0009

TEACHING INTERESTS
Secondary School Theatre Instructor and Technical Director

TEACHING EXPERIENCE
Mankato State University, Mankato, Minnesota, 1986-1988
Teaching Assistant. Responsible for laboratory courses, teaching
appropriate techniques and evaluating student projects and performance.
Supervised production crews in set construction, stagecraft, lighting, and sound.

RELATED EXPERIENCE
Technical Director, Designer, and Production Coordinator, for eight high
school dramatic productions and three musicals, at St. Agnes High School,
Academy of the Holy Angels, and DeLasalle High School (Twin City area
schools). Taught stagecraft skills to high school students and supervised
student production crews (1990-1993).

PROFESSIONAL EXPERIENCE
Chimera Theatre, St. Paul, Minnesota, 1992-present
Production manager, responsible for recruiting technicians, including
volunteers, coordinating all technical crews, maintaining production
schedules, and overseeing production budgets.

Old Log Theatre, Excelsior, Minnesota, 1989-1991
Technician, with responsibilities in lighting, sound, and rigging; **Lighting Designer**,
twelve productions, **Sound Designer**, eight productions, **Set Designer**, three productions.

Paul Bunyan Playhouse, Bemidji, Minnesota, Summers, 1986-1989
Various technical responsibilities in set construction, stagecraft, lighting,
and sound; **assistant stage manager** for two productions, 1988; **stage
manager** for three productions, 1989.

Complete list of production credits available on request.

EDUCATION
Mankato State University, Mankato, Minnesota
M.A. Theater Arts, 1988
College of St. Catherine, St. Paul, Minnesota
B.A. Speech Communication and Drama, 1986

REFERENCES
Available upon request

17

INTERNATIONAL EDUCATION

JOSEPH LOCKE
221 College Street
Any City, State 12345
(101) 555-0009

OBJECTIVE

Desire overseas position as School Administrator or Director

EDUCATION

Ph.D.	**Educational Administration** University of Idaho, Moscow, Idaho	1988
M.A.	**Secondary Curriculum and Administration** University of Utah, Salt Lake City, Utah	1980
B.S.	**Mathematics and Biology** McKendree College, Lebanon, Illinois	1974

EXPERIENCE SUMMARY

Superintendent	6 years
High School Principal	3 years
Assistant Principal	3 years
Secondary Teacher	6 years

AREAS OF EXPERTISE

Curriculum Development	Staffing	Inservice Training
Community Relations	Budgeting	Negotiations

ADMINISTRATIVE EXPERIENCE

Superintendent, 1992 - present, Gooding Joint District 231, Gooding, Idaho
> K-12 enrollment of 1,076, instructional staff of 72, non-teaching staff of 29.
> Sixty-two percent of graduating seniors attend postsecondary institutions.

Superintendent, 1989-1992, Meadows Valley District 11, New Meadows, Idaho
> School district enrollment of 225

High School Principal, 1985-1988, Rich High School, Randolph, Utah
> School district enrollment of 535; 130 students in high school

Assistant Principal, 1982-1985, Morgan High School, Morgan, Utah
> School district enrollment of 1,750; 485 students in high school

TEACHING EXPERIENCE

Secondary mathematics teacher and basketball coach:
    1978-1980, Morgan High School, Morgan, Utah
    1976-1978, The American School of Barcelona, Barcelona, Spain
    1974-1976, Aledo Community School District 217, Aledo, Illinois

TRAVEL & LANGUAGES

Extensive travel in Spain, France, Italy, Greece, North Africa. Good comprehension and speaking ability in Spanish, reading knowledge of French.

CIVIC ACTIVITIES

Board member, Gooding County United Way, 1994 - present
Founding member, Gooding Area Conservation Project, 1993 - present
Executive committee, New Meadows Youth Organization, 1991-1993

PROFESSIONAL MEMBERSHIPS

American Association of School Administrators
Idaho Association of School Administrators

PERSONAL INFORMATION

Married (to licensed elementary teacher); two daughters, ages 14 and 11
U.S. citizen

PLACEMENT FILE

References available from Career Planning and Placement, Any City, State 12345
Telephone: (101) 555-0008   FAX: (101) 555-0089

PAULA RAYE

Present Address:	Stateside Address:
International School of Brussels	221 College Street
19 Kattenberg	Any City, State 12345
1170 Brussels, Belgium	(101) 555-0009 - parents' phone
(322) 555-67-27	

TEACHING EXPERIENCE

1993 - present
International School of Brussels, Brussels, Belgium
Elementary Teacher, Grades 3 and 4
Teach science and mathematics; team teach social studies and language arts; create learning centers for math and science activities with emphasis on developing higher order thinking strategies.

1990-1993
Faulkton Elementary School, Faulkton, South Dakota
Elementary Teacher, in self-contained Grade 3 classroom; responsible for instruction in all subjects except music.

1986-1990
Shaktoolik Elementary School, Bering Strait School District, Shaktoolik, Alaska
Elementary Teacher, Grades 4 and 5

1978-1986
Loneman School Corporation, Oglala, South Dakota
Elementary Teacher, Grade 4 (3 years), Grade 3 (5 years)

EDUCATION

1985
Master's Degree in Elementary Education
University of South Dakota, Vermillion, South Dakota

1978
Bachelor's Degree in Education
Sinte Gleska College, Rosebud, South Dakota

FAMILY INFORMATION

Married; husband is a secondary science teacher and coach
One daughter, age 3
United States citizen

REFERENCES

Credentials available from Teacher Education Center
Any City, State 12345   (101) 555-0008

JAN SILBERS

221 College Street	Any City, State 12345	(101) 555-0009

EDUCATIONAL BACKGROUND:

English Education
University of Delaware

Master of Arts   1993
Newark, Delaware

English/History
Delaware State College

Bachelor of Arts   1991
Dover, Delaware

PROFESSIONAL EXPERIENCE:

English Teacher, Newark High School, Newark, Delaware
Current responsibilities include teaching general English (grade 11), American Authors survey course (grade 12), and an advanced composition course (grade 12). Developed curriculum for composition course, designed and implemented learning centers for general English, and served on textbook selection committee for the authors course.

STUDENT TEACHING:

Dover Air Force Base Middle School, Dover, Delaware
Spring 1991. Taught two sections of basic English (grade 7) and one section of American History (grade 8). Designed tests and evaluated student progress, participated in open house for parents, and organized field trip to State Capitol Building. Experience with large and small groups and individual instruction.

TRAVEL ABROAD:

Co-Sponsor, Newark Area High Schools Tour of France   1993
Toured Southern Europe and North Africa   Summer 1990
AFS Student, Orleans, France   Junior Year 1986

LANGUAGE COMPETENCIES:

French - excellent reading and writing skills, good conversational ability
Spanish - reading knowledge

HONORS:

Graduated with highest honors, Delaware State College   1991
Awarded the President's Young Scholar Certificate   1991

PROFESSIONAL AFFILIATIONS:

Phi Delta Kappa
Delaware Education Association
National Council of Teachers of English

SPECIAL INTERESTS:

Tennis, photography, classical music, cooking, stamp collecting, traveling

CITIZENSHIP & MARITAL STATUS:

U.S.A.
Single, no dependents

CREDENTIALS AVAILABLE:

Career Planning & Placement Office
Any City, State 12345
Telephone: (101) 555-0008   FAX: (101) 555-0089

SARAH LEVINE

221 College Street
Any City, State 12345 USA
(101) 555-0009

OBJECTIVE

ESL Teacher in Japan

Personal attributes include honesty, courtesy, responsibility, punctuality, and fairness.

EDUCATION

College of William and Mary, Williamsburg, Virginia
B.A. Degree - June 1995
Double Major: English and Philosophy

COURSE HIGHLIGHTS

Modern English Grammar	Psychology of Teaching
American Writers	Philosophy East and West
Women in Literature	Ancient Philosophy Seminar

EXPERIENCE

Teaching Related:

English Tutor, Academic Center, College of William and Mary
September 1994 - May 1995

Temporary English Test Specialist, College Testing Program
Washington, D.C. fall semester 1993

Travel:

Extensive travel in Canada, Mexico, and United States
Participated in 1993 Black Hills summer archeological dig

Language:

Native English speaker
Spanish, read and write and speak (5 semesters)
Japanese (2 semesters)

COLLEGE ACTIVITIES

Student Alumni Association
College Flute Choir
Delta Delta Delta (Chair, Community Service)
Student Volunteer, Hospice Road Races
Volunteer Worker, Oakdale Nursing Home

CREDENTIALS

Academic Support Services, Any City, State 12345
Telephone: (101) 555-0008   FAX: (101) 555-0089

IVAN KARLSSON
221 College Street
Any City, State 12345
(101) 555-0009 (home)
(101) 545-0005 (school)

TEACHING OVERVIEW:

Overseas: 4 years
    International School of Stavanger
    Jakarta International School

Stateside: 8 years
    New Trier Township High School District #203, Wilmette, Illinois
    Broward County Public Schools, Ft. Lauderdale, Florida

ACADEMIC BACKGROUND:

Florida International University, Miami, Florida
    Ph.D. Global Studies 1994-present
The University of London, London, England
    Fulbright Fellowship in Communication Studies, 1991-1992
Stetson University, Orlando, Florida
    Bachelor of Arts Degree in History and English, 1981

Licensure: Permanent Teaching Certificate, State of Florida
Teaching Certificate in History and English, State of Illinois

TEACHING EXPERIENCE:

International School of Stavanger, Stavanger, Norway 1992-1994
    History teacher, International Baccalaureate Program
Nova High School, Broward County Schools, Ft. Lauderdale, Florida 1986-1991
    Honors English, American History, Geography
Jakarta International School, Jakarta, Indonesia 1984-1986
    American History I and II, Advanced Placement American History
New Trier Township High School District #203, Wilmette, Illinois 1981-1984
    Composition, English 10, British Literature I

LEADERSHIP EXPERIENCE:

Department Chair, International School of Stavanger, 1994
    *Responsible for designing master schedule, developing budget
    and working closely with individual faculty members.*
Faculty Representative to European Council of International Schools
Curriculum Roundtable, London, England, 1993
    *One of twenty-five representatives who evaluated, discussed and made
    recommendations regarding curricula in international settings.*
President, Florida State Council for the Social Studies, 1991
    *Presided over a 700 member state organization interested in improving
    social studies education.*

MEMBERSHIPS:

National Council for the Social Studies   Society for History Education
National Council for Teachers of English   Overseas Education Association

GRADUATE ASSISTANTSHIPS:

Teaching Assistant, Social Studies Methods, College of Education,
Florida International University, 1994-present.
Responsibilities include the instruction of two sections of social studies
methods classes for education majors. Evaluated papers and exams and prepared
lectures. Guest speaker in various classrooms about international education.

International Student Liaison, Global Studies Department, Florida International
University, 1994-present.
Assist foreign students with questions or concerns about course requirements
and scheduling, living arrangements, and campus policies. Help new students
cope with culture shock and living adjustments in a foreign culture.

SCHOOL SERVICE:

Chair, Extended Learning Program Committee, Stavanger, Norway, 1993
Member, Headmaster Interview Committee, Stavanger, Norway, 1993
Co-chair, School Improvement Plan Committee, Ft. Lauderdale, 1991
Member, Curriculum Enrichment Committee-Humanities, Ft. Lauderdale, 1989-1991
Inservice Presenter, Humanities in the High Schools, Broward County Schools, 1991
Member, Teacher Selection Committee, New Trier High School, 1983
Member, English Writing Team (state grant), New Trier High School, 1982

TRAVEL:

Extensive travel on four continents. Highlights include backpacking in the
Himalayas, train travel through Siberia, photo safari in Kenya, visiting
archaeological ruins on the island of Lesbos, and sailing the Indian Ocean.

RELEVANT INFORMATION:

U.S. citizen
Married, wife is certified elementary teacher
Two dependents, high school student accompanying parents and college student
attending UCLA.

CURRENT VOLUNTEER AND RELATED EXPERIENCE:

Guest Speaker, international travel and education topics, Miami, Florida
Volunteer Teacher's Aid, Haitian Refugee Center, Miami, Florida
Adult Tutor, Haitian Community Education Center, North Miami, Florida

REFERENCES AVAILABLE UPON REQUEST AT
Placement and Teacher Certification
Any City, State 12345
(101) 555-0008 FAX: (101) 555-1118

LAURA GRAHAM

221 College Street
Any City, State 12345
(101) 555-0009

30 Royal Avenue
Mytown, State 23456
(909) 333-0003

PROFESSIONAL BACKGROUND

Administration:
Principal, Thermopolis Middle School, Thermopolis, Wyoming, 1987-present
   Responsible for administration of a staff of 28 teachers; student body of 420.
   Initiated a parent advisory committee; initiated regular newsletter to improve communication
   with parents. Chaired local continuing education committee.

Assistant Principal, Rawlins High School, Rawlins, Wyoming, 1983-1987
   Duties included discipline, attendance, behavioral conferences and class and staff scheduling.

Counseling/Teaching:
Head Counselor, Wyoming Girls' School, Sheridan, Wyoming, 1980-1982
Counselor/Family Living Teacher, 1977-1980, and Home Economics Teacher, 1971-1975,   Sheridan
High School, Sheridan, Wyoming

ACADEMIC TRAINING

University of Wyoming	1982-1983	Ed.S. Educational Administration
Laramie, Wyoming	1975-1977	M.A. Counseling
University of Maine	1967-1969	B.S. Home Economics:
Orono, Maine		Family Studies emphasis
Husson College	1965-1969	Psychology
Bangor, Maine		

PROFESSIONAL MEMBERSHIPS

National Association of Secondary School Principals
University of Wyoming Committee for Friends of Foreign Students
American School Counselors Association
Women in Educational Leadership

LANGUAGE AND TRAVEL

Bilingual - Spanish/English
Traveled extensively in the United States, Mexico and Central America

PERSONAL DATA

Born in Sabattus, Maine; married to free-lance writer/photographer; no dependents

REFERENCES

College of Education Career Services, Any City, State 12345
Telephone: (101) 555-0008   FAX: (101) 555-0089

TEACHERS IN CANADA

ELLEN MORGAN

PRESENT ADDRESS (until April 30)	PERMANENT ADDRESS
12 Jane Street	75 Bloor Street
Some City, Province	Town, Province
(100) 734-2000	(100) 723-1000

EDUCATION

Bachelor of Education
Four-year Concurrent Program
Primary-Junior Divisions

Queen's University
Kingston, Ontario
1995

Bachelor of Arts
Psychology, Mathematics

Trent University
Peterborough, Ontario
1994

O.S.S.H.G.D.
Falls, Spring '92

Morning Star Secondary School
Mississauga, Ontario
1990

ADDITIONAL QUALIFICATIONS

Reading, Part 1

Queen's University
Summer 1995

Sign Language (Beginners)

St. Joseph Hearing Centre
Peterborough, Ontario
1993

Grade 8 Piano
Grade 2 Theory

Royal Conservatory of Music
Toronto, Ontario
1989

TEACHING EXPERIENCE

Grade 1, 4/5
*taught all subjects, supervised
extracurricular activities,
organized field trips, designed
15 units, attended staff
meetings and, in general, assumed
responsibilities of regular staff
member*

Cedar Heights Public School
Peterborough, Ontario
January to April 1995
4 month internship

Grade 3
math, language arts

Centennial Public School
Kingston, Ontario
October 1994, 2 weeks

Grades 1, 3, 4, 5, 6, 8
*taught all subjects at these
grade levels during
undergraduate program*

Several schools in Peterborough
1991-1994
6 weeks total

RELATED EXPERIENCE

Teacher's Aide
*worked with eight developmentally
delayed 4-7 year old pupils to
prepare them for integration
into regular classes*

Grove School
Peterborough, Ontario
1993-94, 2 hours per week

Swimming Instructor
*taught beginners and intermediate
level groups ages 5-12*

Westhaven Recreation Centre
Mississauga, Ontario
Summers 1992-94

OTHER EXPERIENCE

Waitress, campus security patrol, cashier

EXTRACURRICULAR ACTIVITIES

University: Varsity swim team, course evaluation committee
High School: Student council, yearbook, track team

OTHER INTERESTS

Crafts: rughooking, knitting, needlepoint
Sports: waterskiing, volleyball, cycling
Travel: coast to coast in Canada, extensively through Europe

REFERENCES

Professor Ralph Smarts
Faculty of Education
Queen's University
Kingston, Ontario
K7L 3N6
(613) 547-0000

Ms. Jane Calhoun, Principal
Cedar Heights Public School
Box 14
Peterborough, Ontario
M6B 4H2
(705) 600-0000

Professor Amaryllis MacIntosh
Department of Psychology
Trent University
Peterborough, Ontario
N2L 3G1
(705) 885-0000

Mr. John Supervisor
Westhaven Recreation Centre
115 Maxwell Street
Belfountain, Ontario
L5R 2S1
(416) 825-0000

LANDON DAVIES

PRESENT ADDRESS	**PERMANENT ADDRESS**
(UNTIL MAY 1, 1995)	
12 JANE STREET	R. R. # 4
SOME CITY, PROVINCE	LITTLE TOWNE, PROVINCE
Q7P 7H9	Q8X 8I0
(100) 734-2000	(100) 200-3000

EDUCATION

BACHELOR OF EDUCATION INTERMEDIATE-SENIOR PROGRAM PHYSICS, COMPUTERS	FACULTY OF EDUCATION LAKEHEAD UNIVERSITY THUNDER BAY, ONTARIO	1995
BACHELOR OF ARTS (HONOURS) PHYSICS	UNIVERSITY OF WATERLOO WATERLOO, ONTARIO	1994
SECONDARY SCHOOL HONOURS GRADUATION DIPLOMA	KING CITY SECONDARY SCHOOL KING CITY, ONTARIO	1989

TEACHING AND RELATED EXPERIENCE

PHYSICS, COMPUTERS GRADES 9, 11, 12	RICHMOND HILL, ONTARIO AURORA, ONTARIO	1994-95 10 WEEKS TOTAL
TUTOR SCIENCE	WATERLOO CORRECTIONAL FACILITY WATERLOO, ONTARIO	1994-95
VOLUNTEER PLAYROOM SUPERVISOR	HOSPITAL FOR SICK CHILDREN TORONTO, ONTARIO	WINTER 1991
COACHING	SMITH COLLEGE RUGBY WATERLOO, ONTARIO	1989-90
COUNSELLOR	Y.M.C.A. GORMLEY, ONTARIO	WINTER 1985-86
SUPERVISOR OF ARTS AND CRAFTS PROGRAM	Y.M.C.A. OAK RIDGES, ONTARIO	WINTER 1984
FOUNDER OF THE ALCOHOL AWARENESS COMMITTEE	KING CITY SECONDARY SCHOOL KING CITY, ONTARIO	1987
VICE PRESIDENT OF STUDENT ATHLETIC COUNCIL	KING CITY SECONDARY SCHOOL KING CITY, ONTARIO	1987

ADDITIONAL QUALIFICATIONS

CARDIO-PULMONARY RESUSCITATION	FACULTY OF EDUCATION LAKEHEAD UNIVERSITY	1995
ST. JOHN AMBULANCE FIRST AID	FACULTY OF EDUCATION LAKEHEAD UNIVERSITY	1995
S.C.U.B.A. CERTIFICATE	TIM'S PLACE KING CITY, ONTARIO	1988
ONTARIO ATHLETIC LEADERSHIP CAMP CERTIFICATE	MINISTRY OF EDUCATION LAKE COUCHICHING, ONTARIO	1986

COMPUTER EXPERIENCE

IBM USING MS/DOS WORDPERFECT 5.1, LOTUS 1-2-3	VAX/VMS, UNIX, IBM HEWLETT-PACKARD MAINFRAME SYSTEMS	FORTRAN & BASIC PROGRAMMING LANGUAGES

OTHER EXPERIENCE

LABOURER	KING CITY CONSTRUCTION	SUMMER 1993
LABOURER	JONES LANDSCAPING	SUMMERS 1989-1993

ACTIVITIES AND INTERESTS

SPORTS: RUGBY, FOOTBALL, WRESTLING, TENNIS
OTHER: READING, PHOTOGRAPHY, TRAVEL

REFERENCES

PROFESSOR ALEX SMITH FACULTY OF EDUCATION LAKEHEAD UNIVERSITY THUNDER BAY, ONTARIO L9H 5H8 (100) 200-3300	MR. GARRY MAJERS DEPARTMENT OF GEOGRAPHY KING CITY SECONDARY SCHOOL 100 KING CITY ROAD KING CITY, ONTARIO Q3H 4U3 (150) 130-4444	MR. ALBERT JONES JONES LANDSCAPING 16 MAIN STREET KING CITY, ONTARIO Q1H 8Q9 (150) 130-7890

MAURICE GRESHAM
12 Jane Street
Some City, Province
Q7P 7H9
(100) 734-2000 OR (100) 734-1000

EDUCATION

Bachelor of Education: Junior/Intermediate History. In Progress   University of Toronto

Master of Arts: History. 1990   University of Western Ontario

Honours Bachelor of Arts: Humanities (Great Distinction)   University of Lethbridge (Alberta)

Associate: Speech and Drama. (Correspondence) 1987   Trinity College, London, England

EMPLOYMENT

Teaching Assistant

Western European Integration since 1945. 1992   University of Toronto
20th Century Intelligence and Espionage. 1991   University of Western Ontario
Western Civilisation. 1989/1990

- **Lectured/taught** tutorial classes and discussions
- **Evaluated/graded** student progress, assignments, reports, and examinations
- **Consulted** with faculty regarding course curriculum
- **Advised** students regarding course content (office hours)

English Language Reference Coordinator   Prague, Czechoslovakia

Federal Committee for the Environment. November 1990-July 1991
Department of International Relations

- **Planned/taught** English as a second language (ESL) in a classroom setting
- **Supervised/edited** foreign English language correspondence
- **Edited/revised** ministry documents
- **Liaison** between Czechoslovak government and foreign environment ministries
- **Welcomed/assisted** foreign delegations
- **Participated** in the planning of international conference: Environment for Europe
- **Edited/clarified** all Czechoslovak and conference documents
- **Member** of Czechoslovak delegation in conference sessions
- **Produced/designed/distributed** the document "Conference Conclusions"

Teacher: Speech and Drama (certified)   Lethbridge Community College

Conservatory of Speech. September 1986-June 1989

- **Taught** fundamental elements of speech and drama
- **Conducted** private tutoring/elocution sessions
- **Prepared** students for regional and/or provincial festivals and competitions
- **Rehearsed/directed** various forms of performance and expression (e.g., poetry, acting, mime, storytelling)

Storyteller   Lethbridge, Alberta

Lethbridge Public Library. January 1989-April 1989

- Read stories and folktales to children aged 5 to 12
- Performed in public school classes

169

————————— MAURICE GRESHAM / page 2 —————————

SCHOLARSHIPS, AWARDS, DISTINCTIONS

Academic
- Ontario Graduate Scholarship. 1991
- University of Western Ontario Entrance Scholarship. 1989
- University of Western Ontario Special University Scholarship. 1989, 1990
- Nominee, University of Lethbridge Gold Medal (Arts). 1989
- Louise McKinney Post-Secondary Scholarship. 1988
- University of Lethbridge Scholarship. 1987
- Sven Erickson Citizenship Scholarship for Canadian Studies. 1987
- Dean's Honour List - University of Lethbridge. 1986, 1987, 1988, 1989
- University of Lethbridge Entrance Scholarship. 1985
- Alexander Rutherford Scholarship. 1985

Other
- Lethbridge Music Festival Scholarship. 1987
- Alberta Music Festival, Runner-Up, Senior Speech. 1987
- City of Lethbridge Award. 1985
- Alberta Music Festival Provincial Trophy and Scholarship, Junior Speech. 1985
- Lethbridge Tennis Club Under-19 Champion. 1985

EXTRA-CURRICULAR ACTIVITIES/COMMUNITY INVOLVEMENT

Mentor/Advisor: Afro-Canadian Mentorship Programme
York Region Board of Education. Currently Active

Graduate Representative: OXFAM Canada (Toronto)
University of Toronto. 1991-92

History Department Representative: Society of Graduate Students
Member: Feminist Awareness, Issues, and Rights Committee (FAIR)
University of Western Ontario, 1989-90

Vice-President: University of Lethbridge New Democratic Party (NDP) Club
University of Lethbridge 1989-90

Participant: Challenge '89 Student Business Programme
University of Lethbridge. 1989

Secretary Treasurer: Students Against Nuclear Extinction (SANE)
Vice President: Students Against Nuclear Extinction (SANE)
President: Students Against Nuclear Extinction (SANE)
University of Lethbridge. 1985-1989

Teacher: Lethbridge Music Festival
Participant: Lethbridge Music Festival
Lethbridge, Alberta. 1987-89. 1973-89.

REFERENCES

Available on Request

170

ADRIENNE POMEROY
12 Jane Street
Some City, Province
Q7P 7H9

Telephone: (100) 734-2000

TEACHING EMPLOYMENT

1989-present	**THE RURAL DAY SCHOOL** Towne, Ontario Teacher of grade 6 homeroom, grades JK - 8 vocal music. Extracurricular activities include remedial work, direction of choir, soloists, programmes in drama, musical theatre and dance.
1988-1989	**DUFFERIN PRIVATE SCHOOL** Yorkton, Ontario Teacher of core French, grades 7-10 Extracurricular activities included French club and assistance in musical theatre productions.
1985-1987	**ELM STREET ELEMENTARY SCHOOL** Elmwood, Saskatchewan Teacher of vocal music grades 1-6. Languages of instruction were French and English. Extracurricular activities included primary, junior and boys' choirs, solo voice instruction and drama.
1980-1984	**Y.M.C.A. CAMP** Toronto, Ontario Camp director and instructor. Responsible for staff management and co-ordination and implementation of activities program.

EDUCATION

1983-1984	DALHOUSIE UNIVERSITY One-year Teacher Certification	
1978-1983	UNIVERSITY OF WINDSOR Bachelor of Arts, French and Music	
1977-1978	SOUTH TORONTO COLLEGIATE Secondary School Honours Graduation Diploma	

ADDITIONAL QUALIFICATIONS AND INTEREST COURSES

1992   YORK UNIVERSITY
Drama, Part 1

1991   UNIVERSITY OF TORONTO
Honour Specialist, Music

1990-1991   YORK UNIVERSITY
French as a Second Language, Part 1

1987-1988   GEORGE BROWN COLLEGE
Culinary Arts

1984   UNIVERSITY OF PRINCE EDWARD ISLAND
French Immersion Classroom Methods

1977   UNIVERSIDAD DE SALAMANCA, Spain
Spanish Language and Culture

TRAVEL   United Kingdom, Spain, France, Switzerland, Mexico,
United States of America and Canada

LANGUAGES   Fluent in English, French and Spanish

INTERESTS   Travel, folklore, cooking, cycling, cross country running,
reading, music and theatre

SKILLS   Experience with Macintosh, Atari and IBM personal
computers for word processing, marks, report cards,
inventory and music composition
Driver's license

ROBERT MacDOUGALL

12 Jane Street
Some City, Province
Q7P 7H9
(100) 723-2000 [Res]
(100) 723-1000 [Bus]

PROFESSIONAL EXPERIENCE

The Canuck County School District
The Maplewood School District
1975 - present

Social Studies
and
Language Teacher

- Established World Issues course for Senior Secondary in 1982 and taught it each year since. Assisted with set up of student environmental group HOPE (Helping Our Planet's Environment) in 1989.

- Acquired skills in organizing and presenting material to students from many different backgrounds and with a wide range of abilities (basic level to advanced level). Organized courses of study in the geography of Europe, Asia, Canada and Australia. Taught all grades from 9 to 12 at all levels. Motivated students to take further training for careers in urban planning, environmental studies and geography. Member of Grade 9 writing team for a general level geography course; also taught Intermediate Math, English and History.

Adult Class
French Instructor

- Organized and presented a course in World Issues for adult evening classes.

Coach - Boys' Sports

- Coached successful teams in cross-country running and soccer

Professional
Interests

- Teaching Senior Social Sciences
- Teaching Geography to Senior Secondary
- Further overseas teaching opportunities
- Study of education outside North America

LEADERSHIP PROFILE

Exchange Teacher

- Taught in Scotland for the academic year 1987-88. Travelled throughout Eastern and Western Europe including France and U.S.S.R.

Teachers' Union

- Teachers' Union Communications Committee, June 1983. Appointed to three year term, June 1984

Curriculum
Assistant

- Presented workshop to school administration and department heads on incorporating Complex Skills in course material. Assisted teachers in preparing courses which reflected school district and Ministry expectations (1982-1984)

ROBERT MacDOUGALL - Page Two

EDUCATIONAL AND PROFESSIONAL TRAINING

Master of Arts

University of Manitoba
Major Area: Political Science
Minor Area: Statistics and Government
Awarded McMillan Scholarship to cover tuition and expenses during graduate studies (1975).

Bachelor of Arts
(Honours)

Laurentian University, Sudbury (1972)
Major Area: Economics
Area of Concentration: Political Science

Professional

Bachelor of Education, Faculty of Education
University of Toronto (1973)

Honours Specialist Course: Geography and Economics
Faculty of Education, Queen's University (1978)
Completed eight university geography courses, as part of a personal upgrading plan, at various universities (McGill, Queen's, Trent)

English as a Second Language, Part 1 (1992)
Special Education, Part 1 (1986)
Guidance, Part 1 (1985)
Principal's Course, Part 1 (1982)
Junior Division (1991)

OTHER ACHIEVEMENTS

Appointment

Ministry of Education Thinking Skills Project
As team member received specialized training to promote excellence in learning skills

Award

Canuck School District Distinguished Service Award

Exchange

Selected for international exchange program

RECREATIONAL INTERESTS

Cycling, jogging
Study and travel overseas
Railway Modelling
Member, Environmental Resource Association

REFERENCES AVAILABLE UPON REQUEST

RHONDA LAURENCE
12 Jane Street
Some City, Province
Q7P 7H9
(100) 734-2000

EDUCATION

Bachelor of Education Intermediate Senior Divisions Visual Arts, English	Faculty of Education Queen's University Kingston, Ontario	1995
Bachelor of Fine Arts Honours Most Outstanding Woman Artist Award	School of Art York University Toronto, Ontario	1983

SPECIAL SKILLS

- Painting, drawing, and printmaking in all media
- Sculpture in all media, including installations
- Crafts, with emphasis on pottery
- Design, especially graphics, layout and calligraphy
- Basic video production
- Art history, including women and racial minority artists in western culture
- Professional skills for artists: marketing, grants, and proposals
- Exhibition curating, jurying, and reviewing
- Computer graphics and word processing

TEACHING AND RELATED EXPERIENCE

Practice Teaching **Visual Arts, English**	Claude Watson Arts Program Earl Haig Secondary School North York, Ontario	Spring 1995 Four weeks
Media Production, English Grades 11A, 12B, 12G	Prince Edward Collegiate Picton, Ontario	Fall 1994 Two weeks
Visual Arts Grades 9G, 10A	Centre Hastings S.S. Madoc, Ontario	Fall 1994 Two weeks
Creative Artist in Schools Taught sixteen visual arts programs sponsored by the Ontario Council	Eastern Ontario elementary and secondary schools	1983-95
Courses, Lectures, and Symposia **(detailed listing provided on request)** Numerous courses and workshops taught in visual arts (painting, sculpture, pottery, design, colour theory, drawing) for adults and children.	Guilds, museums, galleries, community colleges, universities, and community centres across Ontario and in Alberta, Quebec and Nova Scotia.	1978-95
Art Resource for Lanark County Schools Activities include writing sculpture curriculum at Board level, providing teacher in-service workshop, organizing an Arts Day; jurying student exhibitions; judging essay writing contests; conducting workshops for teachers and students in storytelling, puppetry, illustration, and mask making.	Lanark County Board of Education Perth, Ontario Elementary schools in the Lanark area working with grades K-8	1990-95

EXHIBITIONS

Recent Solo:

Riverbed	White Water Gallery Sudbury, Ontario	1993
Ad Infinitum/Circle of Fire	Brock University St. Catharines, Ontario	1992
Time Bandits	Olga Harper Toronto, Ontario	1991

Selected Invitational/Juried:

A Propos: Architectural Proposals for Craft	Ontario Crafts Council • provincial travelling exhibition	1993
4x4x4	Cartwright Gallery Vancouver, British Columbia • national travelling exhibition	1992-93
East/West	Memorial University Gallery St. John's, Newfoundland • Ontario-Newfoundland exchange	1991

GRANTS AND AWARDS

Best in Show Award	Lanark Arts Council	1994
Crafts Grants	Ontario Arts Council	1990-94
Materials Assistance Grants	Ontario Arts Council	1990-95
Performance Project Grant	Canada Council	1992
Artists With Their Work Grant	Canada Council	1991

PROFESSIONAL ORGANIZATIONS

Eastern Ontario Arts Advisory Committee	1988-present
Canadian Artists Representation (CARFAC)	1988-present
Visual Arts Ontario	1984-present
Theatre Ontario	1984-present
Ontario Arts Council	1982-present

REFERENCES SUPPLIED ON REQUEST

CATHERINE AMIS

12 Jane Street
Some City, Province
Q7P 7H9
(100) 734-2000

EDUCATIONAL QUALIFICATIONS

Master of Education - 1985
Teaching of English as a Second Language
UNIVERSITY OF BRITISH COLUMBIA
Vancouver, British Columbia, Canada

Bachelor of Education - 1980
UNIVERSITY OF ALBERTA
Edmonton, Alberta Canada

OVERSEAS TEACHING EXPERIENCE

MUNICH INTERNATIONAL SCHOOL, 1993-1995
Munich, Germany
Teacher of middle school language arts and social studies

SICHUAN INSTITUTE OF FOREIGN LANGUAGES, 1989-1990
Chongquing, People's Republic of China
Teacher of English and Methodology

COLEGIO NUEVA GRANADA, 1985-1988
Bogota, Colombia
Teacher of Grades 3, 4

CANADIAN TEACHING EXPERIENCE

MOUNTAIN VIEW PUBLIC SCHOOL, 1990-1993
Calgary, Alberta
Teacher of grade 5 and ESL

OVERLAND PUBLIC SCHOOL, 1980-1985
Stettler, Alberta
Teacher of grades 2, 3, 4

RELATED EXPERIENCE

ST. JOHN'S ANGLICAN CHURCH, 1975-1989
Eganville, Alberta
Sunday School Teacher, grades 1 and 2

SUMMER DAY NURSERY SCHOOL, 1975-1977 (Summers)
Lampton, Alberta
Ages 3-5

EXTRACURRICULAR

Speech Festival, Poetry Recital, Drama Club, Yearbook,
Field Hockey, Recycling Club

OTHER INTERESTS

Travel: Across Canada, China, Japan, Germany, Austria, Colombia,
Venezuela

Sports: Aerobics, Ice Skating, Cycling, Sailing, Swimming

Other: Languages, Photography, Reading, Movies

PERSONAL BACKGROUND

Canadian Citizen, single, excellent health

REFERENCES

Please see attached letters, others on request

ELAINE KINSETT

12 Jane Street
Some City, Province
Q7P 7H9
(100) 734-2000

SUMMARY OF QUALIFICATIONS

- Degrees in Arts, Library Science and Education
- Twenty years' professional experience in university, college and secondary school settings
- Well-developed skills in the areas of supervision, automation, and project management

EDUCATION

- M.Ed., Education - Curtin University, Australia, 1993
- B.Ed., Education - Queen's University, 1977
- Ontario Teacher's Certificate, 1977
- B.L.S., Library Science - University of Toronto, 1970
- B.A., English and Latin - Queen's University, 1969

PROFESSIONAL EXPERIENCE

Carleton Board of Education, Ottawa, Ontario
09/85 to Present
Teacher/Librarian.   Resource teacher for a large secondary school. Duties include instruction in research methods, planning and implementation of automation projects, curriculum consultation, and administration of the Library Resource/Centre. Equipment used includes Macintosh and Apple II networks, IBM and Vax configurations, modem access to local and distant databases. In 1987 the Library established the first secondary school CD-ROM facility in Carleton County, which has now grown to three workstations and twelve databases.

Algonquin College of Applied Arts & Technology, Ottawa, Ontario
08/82 to 08/85
Manager of Media, Technical and Audio-Visual Equipment Services.
Directed all centralized services of the Resource Centre that provided technical and specialized support to ongoing college operations. Supervised twenty-six staff in six service areas. Prepared policy, planning and briefing documents and was responsible for a budget of two million dollars. Supervised the College's Media Production (publishing and graphic arts) section. Special projects included automation of cataloguing, remote ordering, and equipment control as well as office automation. Became familiar with IBM 3101 mainframe, DOBIS/LIBIS software, TRS microcomputers, and a word processing network.

Queen's University, Kingston, Ontario
07/77 to 08/82
Principal Librarian. Established a Bibliographic Instruction program for the University Library. This includes planning and development as well as liaison with student government, faculty and university administrators. Teaching methods employed were self-instruction via videotape, research seminars, term paper clinics, credit assignments. Duties included staff training and program evaluation. Concurrently, I was Reference Librarian providing user assistance and performing searches of automated remote databases such as QL, BRS, INFO-GLOBE, and Dialog.

Queen's University, Kingston, Ontario
07/74 to 06/77
Head of Technical Processing, Education Library. Duties involved technical back-up to users of the Faculty of Education print collection, including cataloguing, acquisitions and supervision of five staff members.

Conseil Scolaire Regional de Tilly, Ste. Foy, Quebec
10/73 to 06/74
School Librarian. Provided library service to students, staff and administrators of a large urban secondary school.

Cornwall Public Library, Cornwall, Ontario
07/70 to 07/73
Children's Librarian. Provided children's programming and community services by school visits, story hours, puppet shows, etc. I chose, displayed and promoted materials and service to the clientele.

OTHER RECENT PROFESSIONAL ACTIVITIES AND INTERESTS

- Member of two provincial committees for teacher education (OTF, OECTA)

- Member of Apple Library Users Group (A.L.U.G.)
- Executive member of local teacher affiliate

- Experience on Affirmative Action Committees, Salary Evaluation Committee, Provincial Administrative Staff Association, Senate Budget Review Committee (Queen's).

- Participant in short courses and workshops on microcomputers, library automation, leadership

- Sabbatical year, 1991-92, travel and study/research in France and Australia

- Overseas Postgraduate Research Scholarship (Commonwealth of Australia) Recipient, 1991

- O.E.C.T.A. Scholarship Recipient, 1991

EVAN CORWIN

HOME ADDRESS: 12 Jane Street
Some City, Province
Q7P 7H9
(100) 734-2000

SCHOOL ADDRESS: Valleyfield Elementary and High School
3600 Some Street
Small City, Province
Q7P 7H8
(100) 734-3000

ADMINISTRATIVE AND TEACHING EXPERIENCE:

1991-1995   VALLEYFIELD ELEMENTARY AND HIGH SCHOOL
Trois Riviéres, Quebec
Principal and Teacher of Secondary English, School of 400 students K-12

1984-1988   AMHERST AREA HIGH SCHOOL
Port Cove, Nova Scotia
Teacher and Vice Principal

1978-1984   AMHERST AREA HIGH SCHOOL
Port Cove, Nova Scotia
Teacher and Department Head

ACADEMIC QUALIFICATIONS:

1988   LEADERSHIP TRAINING IN EDUCATION
National Centre for Education
Winnipeg, Manitoba

1986   DIPLOMA IN EDUCATIONAL ADMINISTRATION
Nova Scotia Summer School
Halifax, Nova Scotia

1984   MASTER IN EDUCATION, CURRICULUM STUDIES
University of Nova Scotia
Halifax, Nova Scotia

1977   BACHELOR OF EDUCATION
St. Francis Xavier University
Antigonish, Nova Scotia

1976   BACHELOR OF ARTS, ENGLISH/HISTORY
St. Francis Xavier University
Antigonish, Nova Scotia

PROFESSIONAL ACTIVITIES:

1991-93	Worked with the Faculty of Education at McGill University to provide placement and evaluation of student teachers as the principal of a cooperative school.
1991-92	Attended French immersion programs in the summers of 1991 and 1992.
1989-90	Worked with high school principals of Port Cove school district as a facilitator in the development of the district's in-service program.
1986-88	Member of Provincial Appeals Committee of the Nova Scotia Teachers' Union
1985-86	Represented the Nova Scotia Teachers' Union as a member of the Minister's Advisory Committee recommending changes to the Nova Scotia High School Curriculum.

PUBLICATIONS:

"Administrator Burnout," The Canadian School Administrator, Vol. 6, No. 10, May, 1988.

"Electronic Communications Among Schools," Journal of Education, Vol. 4, No. 8, October 1986.

COMMUNITY INVOLVEMENT:

1980-present	Member of Rotary Club
1978-92	Coaching of youth softball and soccer teams
1980-84	Halifax Symphony Association
1978-84	President, Treasurer of Port Cove Recreation Centre

REFERENCES:

Mr. Harvey Loviston
Director General
Valleyfield School District
3600 Some Street
City, Province
Q1S 3R2
(100) 200-1000

Mr. William Wilson
Superintendent of Schools
Amherst School District
P.O. Box 16
City, Province
Q3T 5S9
(100) 200-3000

A FINAL WORD ABOUT RESUMES

Skimming through even a few of the hundred and one résumés presented in this book should make it a bit easier for you to confront the task of writing your own. Of course, a résumé is vitally important if you are looking for employment, but even if you have no urgent or immediate need for it, the time you spend creating a résumé is time well spent.

Whether you are constructing your very first résumé or just updating one that has served you well in the past, take full advantage of the opportunity to record and describe your accumulated experiences and achievements. Your résumé is a professional record of real consequence. It is not just a factual statement of dates and places but an account of genuine significance that can chart progress toward goals, point to authentic abilities, suggest skills to update or strengthen, and even propose new avenues to explore. For this reason alone, any teacher can benefit from preparing a résumé and cultivating the habit of periodic updating and revision.

Although it is not a magic key, a good résumé can open doors that would otherwise remain closed to you. As a means of introduction, it can help you through the employment process, support your efforts to secure funding or grants for special projects, or highlight your particular strengths and skills for leadership roles or positions.

When the time comes to submit your résumé, you can revise, rearrange, and rework the information to make it directly relevant to your specific purpose. Revising and adapting are important processes, but they are only a means to an end. You could fiddle forever attempting to find the precise word, the ideal format, the most efficient, striking, pointed, or focused arrangement of categories, not to mention the most attractive layout, the most legible font, and the most appealing paper to convey your message. But eventually your résumé must stand alone. Except for absolute accuracy about dates and locations, and impeccable spelling and grammar, don't try to be perfect—and don't worry about final versions. As your career develops, your résumé will undergo many changes, many variations. Your goal is not to write the definitive résumé, just a positive, accurate, honest document that establishes and fosters your professional image.

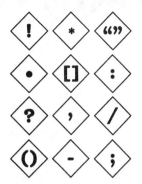